FIG TREE QUILTS

PURINA
SULFAQUINOXALINE MIXTURE

joanna figueroa

FIG TREE QUILTS
fresh vintage sewing

CREDITS

President & CEO • Tom Wierzbicki

Editorial Director • Mary V. Green

Managing Editor • Tina Cook

Development Editor • Karen Costello Soltys

Technical Editor • Laurie Baker

Copy Editor • Marcy Heffernan

Design Director • Stan Green

Production Manager • Regina Girard

Illustrator • Laurel Strand

Cover & Text Designer • Shelly Garrison

Photographer • Brent Kane

All of the photography for this book
was done in Joanna Figueroa's home.

MISSION STATEMENT

Dedicated to providing quality products and
service to inspire creativity.

Fig Tree Quilts: Fresh Vintage Sewing

That Patchwork Place® is an imprint of
Martingale & Company®.

Martingale & Company
20205 144th Ave. NE
Woodinville, WA 98072-8478 USA
www.martingale-pub.com

Printed in China
14 13 12 11 10 09 8 7 6 5 4 3 2 1

Library of Congress Cataloging-in-Publication Data
Library of Congress Control Number: 2008045658

ISBN: 978-1-56477-894-9

DEDICATION

This book is created in honor of all the women who have come before us, leaving behind a wealth of creative ideas, quilts, and inspiration.

I also want to dedicate this to my husband, Eric, and my three kids, Benjamin, Zachary, and Ella. It is largely for them that I work to create my own Fresh Vintage home.

ACKNOWLEDGMENTS

My thanks go to:

Moda Fabrics for their consistent and flawless interpretation of my fabric designs into wonderful collections. Without the professionalism, amazing marketing, and design sense of the Moda design team, this would still all be a paper dream. Thank you everyone at Moda and especially Mark, Cheryl, and Lissa. You all are fabulous!

The wonderful team at Martingale & Company—Karen, Mary, Cathy, and Laurie.

My coconspirators and contributors to this book, Jackie Cate of Wren's Nest, Denise Sheehan of The Graceful Stitch, Janis Stob and Margaret Linderman of December's Child, and Diana Johnson of Quilting from Grammy's Attic. Thank you for your wonderful creativity, your unique contributions, and for making the process of creating this book so much fun!

contents

introduction

I believe that there is something very special and unique about working with fabric that is quite different from any other artistic medium. Fabric is tactile and pliable, can be touched, played with, and manipulated, and then used to create a useful, useable, or wearable item. It is saturated with color, and yet soft and supple at the same time. Working with fabric is often described as soothing, therapeutic, and cathartic. I think these are the main reasons that so many people have been and continue to be drawn to quilting and fabric handicrafts over the centuries. We seem to have a deep emotional connection to textiles that we can't explain in words. Working with and manipulating fabric and creating one-of-a-kind items for ourselves and our friends holds a special place in our lives. It is something many of us do a little bit every day.

Sewing is a timeless art and something that every generation reinterprets in its own way, but it still continues and carries on when other artistic pursuits come and go as fads and passing popularities. It is here to stay and we are glad to be a part of that tradition. Staying tied to that history and yet interpreting it for today's home and fashion is what we strive to do with our Fresh Vintage style.

Fresh Vintage™ is our fresh, clean, light, soft-yet-vibrant color aesthetic that is rooted in traditional design and sensibility. Most of our inspirations and design ideas come from vintage items that have been passed down to us or that we have uncovered at local antique shops or flea markets. I can say with all honesty that spending a weekend morning at a flea market is one of my all-time favorite activities. Over the years I have had the pleasure of uncovering numerous treasures that have led to new and unexpected design possibilities. One time

an aqua antique vase with a small floral design was the central color combination at the heart of an entire fabric collection. From the seemingly insignificant object to such a wonderful end product—who would have ever guessed that journey! And yet that is only one small story from so many. The grace of simple construction, an unusual color combination, the layers of age and patina—you never know what might inspire and lead us down the path to another fabric collection, another quilt, another project. Why don't you come down that path with us and see where it might lead you?

This book can be used to start you down the path or to help you continue along a path well worn with your footsteps already. For those of you who are seasoned quilters, who are sewers, who grew up watching your mothers mending clothes and sewing items for the home, these projects will take you back and inspire you to move forward. For those of you who are new to this art and who are experimenting with that wonderful feeling that comes from making handmade items for the first time, these projects offer you a wide array of choices to get you started. Dive into vintage-inspired bed-sized quilts or charming lap throws that will change the entire feel of your room or porch. Dabble in the sewing world by stitching aprons, pillow covers, or wonderful little items for your own home or as gifts that your friends will cherish forever. Immerse yourself in the world of stuffed, sculpted, hand-stitched art, whether it be a fruit, a vegetable, or an enchanting little wren. Start with an entire ensemble or choose a particular category that draws you in. Either way, I hope that any one of these 20 Fresh Vintage projects will take hold of your imagination and lead you into your own creative space.

Joanna

meet the contributors

I think that the collaboration of creative minds is one of the greatest assets that we have as we quilt, sew, and decorate our homes. Looking through books and magazines, attending classes and workshops, exploring art galleries and gift shops, and seeking out the opinions of other creative folks are among the best ways we have to better our own skill and to hone our own creations. Looking at our projects through the eyes of others almost always makes them stronger, deeper, and better. For me looking to the past and reinterpreting vintage quilts and vintage color combinations is at the root of how I work and design, so I am daily studying the creative work of those that came before me.

As I started working on this book, I thought what better way to go about it than to ask a few uniquely creative gals who also enjoy the inspiration of vintage items to join in this new venture. I knew that their work would add something wonderful to my own quilts and make the book a better whole for you to enjoy. Working with these gals has been a wonderful journey and a pleasure, and I think you will truly enjoy the fruits of our work together. We have grouped our projects into five charming thematic ensembles that you can use in their entirety or pick and choose from to add small tidbits of Fresh Vintage goodness to your home. However you choose to use this book, we hope that it brings you joy and satisfaction as you take time to work with your hands.

Jackie Cate

As a child Jackie did lots of embroidery, needlepoint, and various other crafts, but she never learned to sew. About eight years ago, she took a class and learned to quilt and sew all at the same time. She hasn't stopped since! She especially loves handwork, and makes wonderful vintage-inspired pincushions and hand-sculpted items. In addition to creating patterns with Fig Tree Quilts, she has a little company called Wren's Nest Designs where she sells finished pincushions and *objets d'art*. When she's not quilting or crafting, she's busy keeping up with three very active children, helping at their schools, and enjoying time with her wonderfully supportive and patient husband. She also enjoys sharing bits and pieces of her everyday life on her blog at www.wrensnest.typepad.com.

Denise Sheehan

Denise has always enjoyed sewing and various sorts of crafts, but when she started quilting, she knew it was something special. In the beginning, she was a "classaholic," wanting to learn as many techniques and experience as many different quilting styles as possible. Today she still enjoys different styles, but she leans toward vintage and nostalgic designs, and instead of taking classes, she's teaching them. She also designs quilts for her business, A Graceful Stitch (www.agracefulstitch.com). Denise's husband, Dennis, and daughters, Lindsey and Mandy, are her support system. She hopes her daughters will both someday enjoy quilting as much as she does. Denise is currently attending textile design school and hopes to be designing a line of fabrics in the near future.

Janis Stob and Margaret Linderman

This dynamic mother-daughter seamstress-and-quilter team love working together, although they don't really feel like they can call what they do work. They prefer to call it "genetically unavoidable." For them, digging through piles of fabric and trim looking for just the right one has been a trait passed through generations. Mother Margaret says her interest in textiles and design started at age three with sewing doll clothes and doll bedding, and then progressed to paper dolls soon after. She was never satisfied with available options, so even at an early age she created her own paper creations. Daughter Janis's interest in textiles and design started in the scrap pile at her mother's feet. Her first "clients" were her Troll dolls, which she spiffed up in custom-made fancy jackets with sashes. She eventually progressed to creating her own designs for herself and others and is now armed with a degree in Fashion Design from the Fashion Institute of Design and Merchandising. Both women express their love of textiles through teaching and inspiring others to try something new. You can see more of their creative endeavors at www.decemberschild.com.

Diana Johnson

A longtime San Leandro, California, resident, Diana began quilting 20 years ago as a hobby. Her sole reason for initially learning how to quilt was that one day she hoped to make a Double Wedding Ring quilt. Unfortunately, she has not yet accomplished this goal! After several years as a baker and manager of a restaurant, she decided it was time to go into business for herself. In 2001, she invested in a Gammill Longarm Quilting machine, and the next year she started up her own business, Quilting from Grammy's Attic. Today Diana is an award-winning quilter and has created many quilts seen in shows and admired nationwide. She works with many different styles of quilts but is becoming known for her wonderful feather designs, both traditional and allover. She made all of the quilts in this book shine with Fresh Vintage wonder!

fabric and color selection

When selecting fabric for any of the projects in this book, I use premium-quality 100% cotton, purchased at my local quilt shop. Of course, I use primarily Fig Tree fabric collections by Moda Fabrics and believe that Moda has a lot of the best fabrics out on the market, but I will admit to being at least slightly biased! However, any high-quality 100% cotton would be a good choice for your quilting or sewing project.

For quilting I don't wash any of my fabrics, and so assume that the fabric width will provide at least 42" of usable fabric. I don't prewash the fabrics for a couple of reasons; the slightly stiffer texture that the sizing gives the yardage makes it easier to work with, and fabrics that haven't been prewashed will pucker slightly when washed, giving your quilt that wonderful straight-from-granny's-attic feel. If you want to wash your finished quilt, do so in cold water, and then dry it on low heat. The result should be just wonderful for snuggling!

Because I don't wash any of my quilting fabric, I test any fabric that I think might bleed. A black or deep red would most commonly fall into this category. If you're unsure, test the fabric by putting a small swatch of it into a cup of very hot water along with a drop of detergent. After a few minutes, place the swatch on a white paper towel and dab it. If you see any color transfer onto the paper towel during any part of this, use a different fabric. Most often there will no problem.

For projects other than those that you want to see puckered for an aged look, Janis and Margaret suggest that the fabrics used be prewashed in the manner they will be washed later. This applies to clothing, kitchen items, or pillows that you foresee washing regularly. Prewashing ensures that any shrinkage that may occur will happen before the project is made and not after.

For many of the hand-sculpted items, Jackie used hand-dyed, felted wool. Felted wool is available at many quilt shops, but if you would like to make your own, you can use any 100%-wool fabric. Wash the fabric in hot water, and then dry it in a dryer on the hottest setting. The agitation and heat cause the fibers to felt, or compact. Felted wool is perfect to use for small appliqué pieces because it won't fray, and therefore the edges don't need to be turned under.

FIG TREE FABRICS

The projects in this book are grouped around Fig Tree fabric collections. Even though it is likely that you will not be able to find some of these particular fabrics in order to reproduce the exact look, we list the fabric collections here as a resource for you and hope that they will at least give you a point from which to work. *Front Porch Welcome* is created around the "Dandelion Girl" collection. *Harvest Medley* is created around the "A Day in the Country" collection. *Kitchen Comforts* is created around the "Folklorique" collection. *Chocolat et Crème* and *An English Boudoir* are created around the "Allspice Tapestry" collection. Of course, you are always encouraged to use any grouping of similar-feeling fabrics or create your own palette inspired by what speaks to you!

FRESH VINTAGE COLOR

One of the most important things about working with color is knowing what you really like, what inspires you, and to what you are consistently drawn. This might sound like a simple idea, but the truth is that most people, even most quilters, aren't sure what style they like or what color combinations they like, so they struggle to find palettes that please them. To figure out what you like, you need to start training your eyes to see color palettes. Look not only at fabrics, but at home-decorating colors, dishware colors, gift wrap, stationary, clothing, and gift items. Soon enough you will begin to see your own "trends." Don't be afraid of whatever color palettes you're drawn to, whether they are bright or muted. This will be your first step in choosing well for your quilting and sewing projects.

Not everyone will agree with this statement, but I believe a finished quilt will only be as good as the initial color-palette choices. That still leaves a huge

moda
moda
MILK

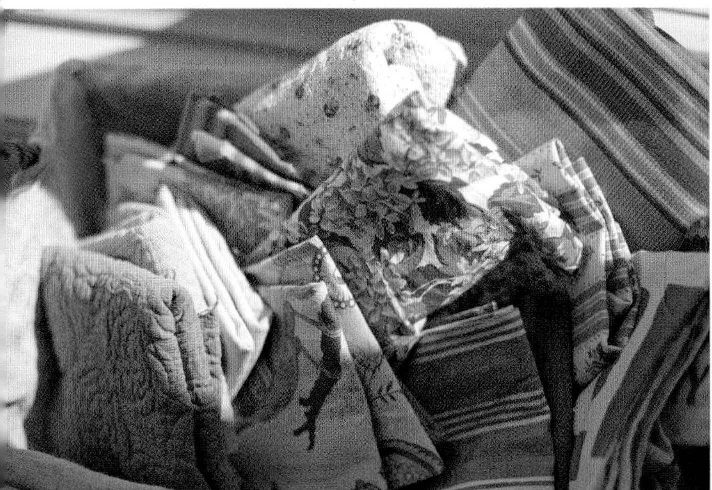

amount of room for interpretation, for color preferences, and for inspiration. But regardless of what kind of color palette you like to work with, the process of choosing your palette is potentially the most important part of the project. Technical expertise is inspiring and amazing to look at, but if you think about what first draws you to a particular quilt or hand-sewn project, your answer will most likely be the color palette or how the colors and fabrics work with one another. There is something about color that affects us each differently. Now having said that, I would like to briefly tell you about my own process of choosing a palette.

I found I could say things with color and shapes that I couldn't say any other way—things I had no words for.

—Georgia O'Keeffe

For me a particular color combination or inspiration is where I always start. The color combinations of old drawings and vintage illustrations have always fascinated me. For whatever reason, we don't often put together such wonderful and unusual combos in this day and age. If you look at illustrations from old children's books, you'll notice that the colors were often just a bit "off," as we would say today, not the color combination that you might expect to see. I love to refer to these colors and palettes as "forgotten" colors because there is just something about them that feels like I'm traveling back to another time. I base all of my fabric collections and quilted projects on these colors, and I hope that they transport you as they do me.

I love to try to capture that vintage feel that often seems so elusive today. To create that palette, whether for a fabric collection or an individual project, I always start with a cream base. What I mean by this is that many fabrics have a white base, making them cooler in appearance. Their basic undertone is white or grey. Some fabrics even have a specifically cool base; there is a blue tone to the color palette. I stay away from those fabrics. Fabrics with a cream base, on the other hand, have cream as their lightest tone and are warmer in general tone and hue. Reds are more tomato reds, orangey and soft. Greens are more limey or chartreuse. Blues are more aqua, with slightly green overtones. Pinks are more likely to be peach and apricot. Even blacks and grays can be warm. You'll be amazed when you start laying black fabrics next to each other and see the amount of difference between a warm and a cool black.

Fabrics often include accent colors that will affect the warm or cool feel of the overall print. Train your eye to look at all the colors in a particular fabric. Look at each color in the color wheel as having the potential to be warm or cool.

Another principle that I often apply is that yellow goes with everything! Many years ago I heard another designer say this in a workshop on bright and contemporary fabrics. The same principle has translated very well into vintage color combinations. There is no color on the color wheel that looks bad with yellow. Think about it. Many of the most classic color combinations are paired with yellow, and yet somehow people seem to be afraid of yellow! Now of course there are many different yellows. The yellows I am talking about are soft butter yellow, or warm mustard yellow, or strong cream yellow. These yellows often form the basis of the color palettes I work with. The strength of the yellow depends on what feeling I am trying to convey or what color combination I am trying to create.

Lastly, I always try to add some colors to "ground" my quilts or projects. Most quilters stay within the medium range of tones, never branching out into true lights or true darks. Personally, I've never struggled with adding cream and ivory as my lights, but adding darks has been another story altogether. Because they are not my favorite colors, I have needed to learn how to add them in successfully. By learning how to add good dark browns, warm blacks, deep plums, and soft grays, I've added a strong grounding element to my designs. These colors give your eyes somewhere to rest as they move around the myriad other colors in your project. They help to give your overall project a more vintage, aged feeling, and they round out your color palette, which strengthens the other color choices you have made. You will be amazed at what a few well-placed taupes or browns can add to an otherwise medium-toned quilt!

Color is my day-long obsession, joy and torment.

—Claude Monet

basic quiltmaking instructions

This section will take you through the basics needed to make the projects in this book. You'll find everything from the basics of rotary cutting to my favorite appliqué techniques, as well as instructions for finishing your quilt.

QUICK CUTTING AND PIECING METHODS

Quick cutting and piecing methods, along with the rotary cutter and the cutting mat, have revolutionized the process of modern-day quilting. Instead of cutting and piecing all the pieces for one block at a time, and then starting all over again for the next block, these methods simplify the process by allowing you to cut and piece identical units for each block at one time. This principle holds true whether the pieces are from a single piece of fabric or 20 different fabrics. If you do the same action over and over again, your pieces will be more accurate, your process will be much faster, and you will reach your goal more quickly.

> **FRESH TIP**
>
> Along your quiltmaking journey, you may encounter patterns that instruct you to cut the pieces for each block and piece them one at a time. As you become more experienced with the quick cutting and piecing methods, it will be easier to modify the instructions so that you can use your time more efficiently.

Rotary Cutting

The instructions for all the quilt projects in this book employ rotary-cutting techniques. You will cut strips first, and then cut across the strip to make squares and/or rectangles as needed for the project. If triangles are needed, squares are cut from strips first, and then the squares are cut in half once or twice diagonally, depending on where the triangle will be used.

1. Begin by straightening one edge of the fabric. To do this, fold the fabric in half lengthwise, aligning the selvage edges. The cut edges along the width of the fabric will most likely be uneven. Lay the fabric on the rotary-cutting mat with the folded edge closest to you. The left edge of the fabric should be lying on the left end of the mat with the excess fabric to your right (reverse this if you're left-handed). Align one edge of a square acrylic ruler along the folded edge of the fabric. Then place a long, straight acrylic ruler to the left of the square ruler so that it just covers the raw edges of the left side of the fabric.

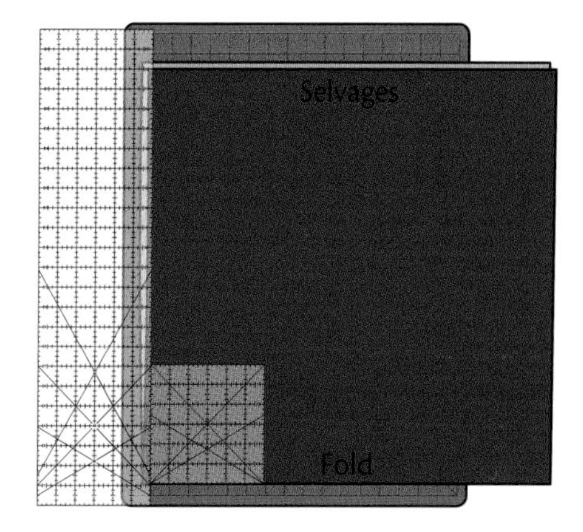

2. With your hand on the long ruler, carefully remove the square ruler. Use the rotary cutter to cut along the right edge of the ruler. Discard the cut piece. You're now ready to cut strips.

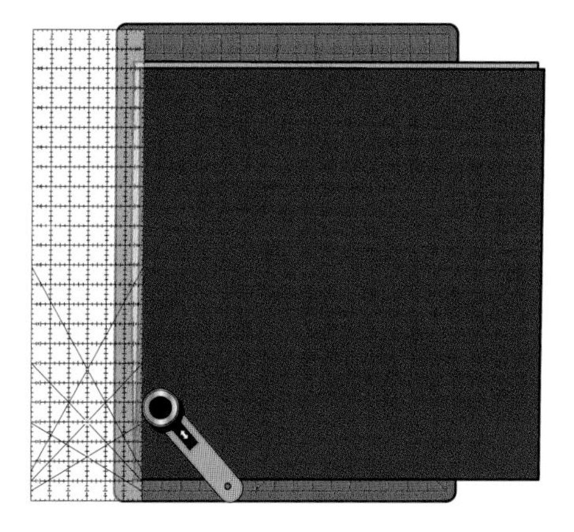

3. Measuring from the straightened edge, cut strips the width given in the pattern instructions. For example, if you need 3"-wide strips, place the 3" vertical line of the ruler on the straightened edge of the fabric and cut along the right edge of the ruler.

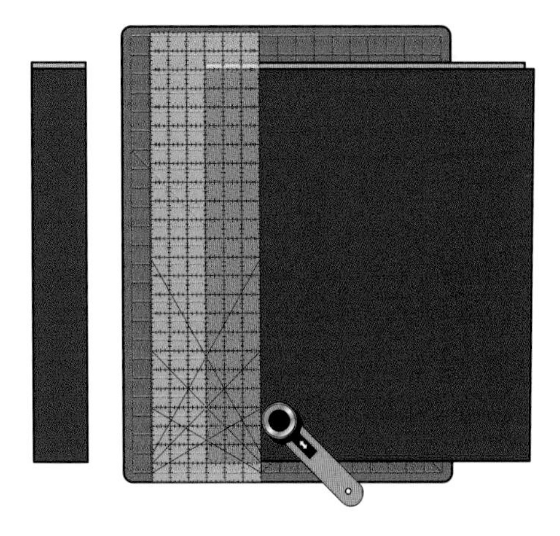

4. To cut squares and rectangles from strips, trim away the selvage ends of the folded strip in the same manner as you did with the whole fabric piece. With the strip still folded, measure the required distance from the straightened end of the strip and cut your piece.

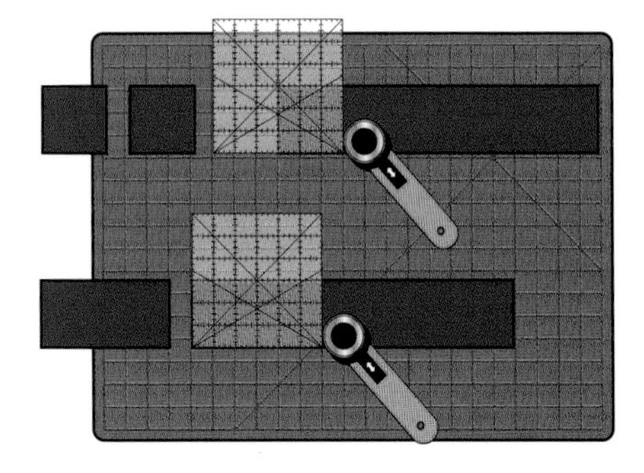

5. To cut triangles, cut a square of the specified size first. If the instructions indicate to cut the square once diagonally, cut from one corner to the opposite corner to yield two half-square triangles. The cut edges are on the bias and should be handled carefully.

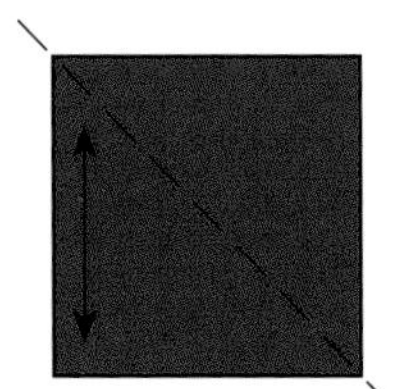

Half-square triangles

If the instructions indicate to cut the square twice diagonally, cut from one corner to the opposite corner in both directions to yield four quarter-square triangles. Again, the cut edges are on the bias.

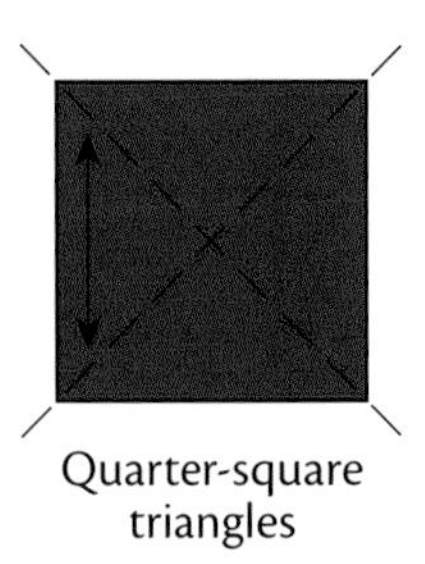

Quarter-square triangles

FRESH TIP

Often I like to dedicate a day or a portion of a day to the process of strip cutting all of my pieces. It feels great when at the end of a single block of time I have cut all the pieces for the entire quilt!

Strip Piecing

Whenever possible, I like to speed up the process of repetitive piecing when I am making block units that have a repeating pattern, such as a checkerboard, nine patch, or rail fence. To do this, sew full-length strips together in the necessary fabric combinations to make a strip set. Press the seam allowances toward the darker fabric or as indicated in the pattern. Then, straighten one end of the strip set and cut it into the desired size segments.

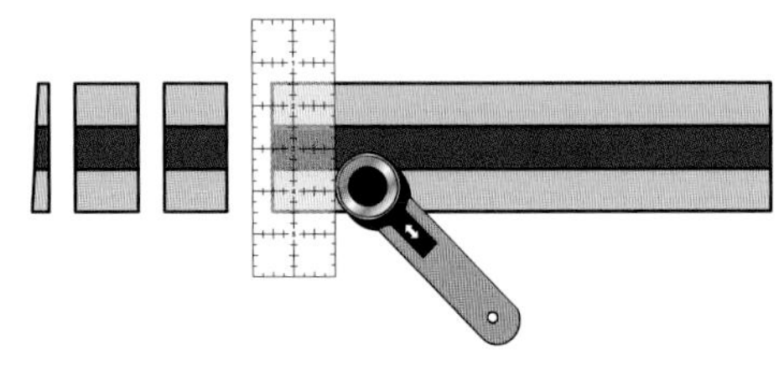

Chain Piecing

Again, this is one of those methods that speeds us through the more tedious phases of the quilting process so that we can more quickly move on to the exciting business of seeing our blocks come together. In this process you simply feed the pieces through your sewing machine one after the other without stopping or cutting threads. After you have finished chain piecing all of one type of unit for your block, remove the chain and snip the threads between the units. Then take the pieces to the ironing board and press as instructed.

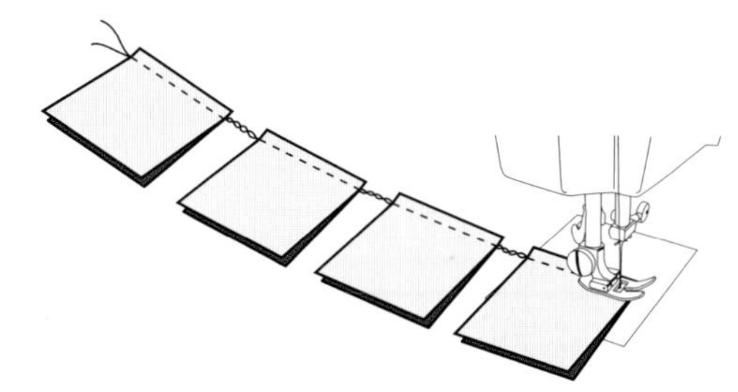

Triangle Units

Another one of my favorite quick-piecing methods involves creating triangles by layering a square onto another square or rectangle, and then sewing diagonally across the smaller square. This folded-corner technique allows you to achieve accurate triangles and bypasses the often troublesome aspect of working with bias edges. I recognize that this method is not always the most economical in terms of fabric, but over the years I have found that it is definitely the most accurate and requires the least amount of extra work.

1. Press the square that will become the triangle in half diagonally, wrong sides together. Open the square and with right sides together, position the pressed square on the larger square or rectangle as indicated in the pattern instructions. Be sure the pressed line is oriented properly. Stitch on the diagonal pressed line.
2. Fold up the top square until its corner matches the corner of the *bottom* piece of fabric, not the piece directly under it, which is the other half of the top square. Press it in place.
3. Trim away only the piece that is the other half of the top square, between the triangle and the bottom layer. Trim 1/4" from the stitching line, leaving the piece of fabric onto which the top square was stitched. If you stitch inaccurately or the pieces shift, the complete bottom piece will create a much more accurate pieced block than if it were cut away.

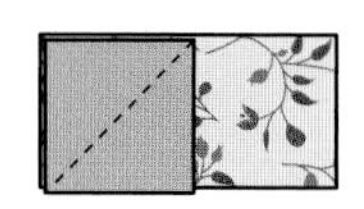

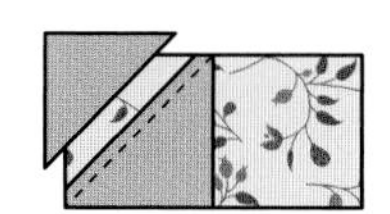

FRESH TIP

A lot of people ask whether leaving the bottom piece creates too much bulk. My answer is always the same; this method is all about piecing more accurately, especially for beginning to intermediate quilters, and the extra layer is seldom a problem.

APPLIQUÉ

I am not an appliqué perfectionist or a meticulously detailed "technique quilter." Normally I do what works best for me in both piecing and appliqué, and I encourage you to do the same. After all, quilting is an art and should be a joy. When it becomes tedious and technical, I think we have lost something central about this medium itself.

In this vein, I don't usually give precise appliqué placement guides in my patterns. I enjoy the freedom of having the pieces given to me in their entirety and putting them together in the way I see fit. When appropriate I do provide placement suggestions, tips, and measurements to assist you in general placement. Never feel like you need to stick to my suggestion to have a successful quilt. I always encourage creativity in all aspects of quilting and this is especially true with appliqué. After all, there's a reason it's called "folk art."

I realize that there are many appliqué methods, but I prefer the starch method when working with cotton fabrics. If you are comfortable with another method, by all means use it. I've also given you some tips for appliquéing with wool.

For any appliqué project, I recommend cutting the background piece about 1" larger all the way around. Often while appliquéing, the background will fray or distort due to stitches drawing in the fabric. By cutting your background piece larger, you have a bit of extra to work with, and you can trim it up when you are done.

Starch Method

For me appliqué was something I endured for the sake of my design until I discovered this method. Although I tried many different methods before this one, none freed me up or gave me the confidence and—yes, I will say it—the desire to work with every kind of appliqué shape in my designs. Since discovering and working to perfect this method, I have grown to love appliqué for the creative design element it adds to the quiltmaking process.

1. Trace one of each of the appliqué patterns onto the *shiny* side of a piece of freezer paper using a fine-point permanent pen or marker. Place this piece on top of a second piece of freezer paper with the shiny side against the dull side of the second piece. Press the two pieces until they are fused together. Cut out the shapes, following the marked lines that you should be able to see through the paper. Basically what this gives you is a doubly strong piece of freezer paper with the image drawn inside, already reversed for you.
2. Iron the freezer-paper shapes you created in step 1, shiny side down, onto the wrong side of the appropriate fabrics, leaving at least ½" of space around each shape and between shapes if more than one will be cut from the same fabric. Cut out the appliqués a scant ¼" beyond the freezer-paper shape. Clip into the seam allowance around curves and on each side of inner points. Sharp curves will need more clips and soft curves will need fewer. Clip a few threads shy of the freezer-paper shape.

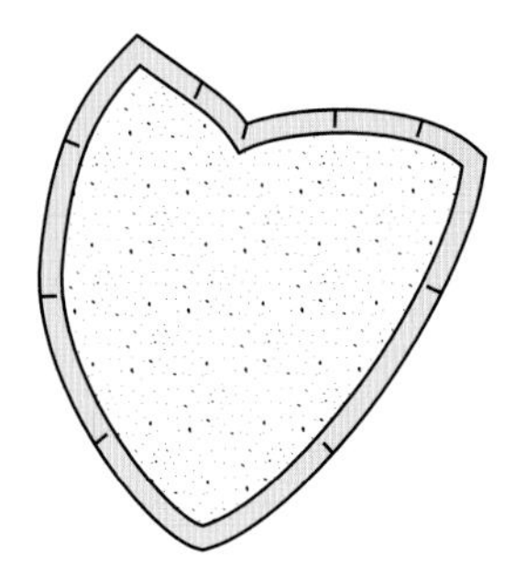

3. Spray some starch into a small jar or the cap of the can and allow the foam to disappear.
4. With the freezer-paper shape still in place and face up, use a small paintbrush to paint the liquid starch onto the entire seam allowance of one of the appliqués.

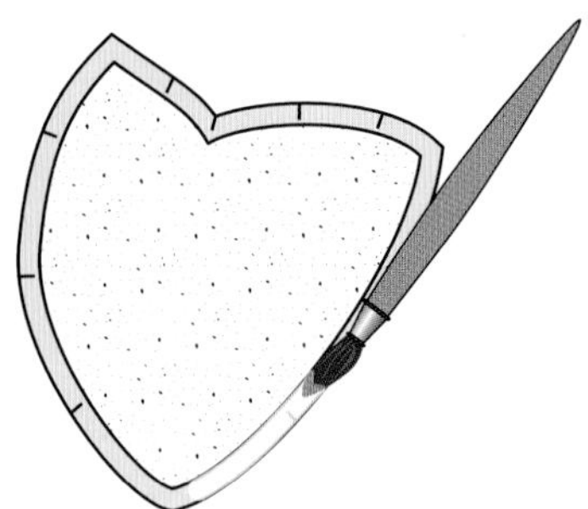

5. Press the seam allowance onto the freezer-paper shape, taking care around corners and curves (see "Fresh Tip" at right for pressing tips). A small iron works well for this task, but a regular household iron will also work. A stiletto is very helpful in pulling the points all the way in as you're ironing down your seam allowance and in generally assisting you with the movement of the fabric as you press.

6. Once the seam allowances are ironed down, pull out the freezer-paper shape and press the shape from the front. Reuse the shape as needed to make additional appliqués. You should be able to make several appliqués before you need a new shape.
7. Repeat steps 4–6 to make any remaining appliqués.

8. Apply small dots of Roxanne's Glue-Baste-It water-soluble glue to the seam allowances on the wrong side of the appliqués; position the appliqués on the background fabric as instructed. Stitch in place by hand using the traditional appliqué stitch described at right or by machine using an invisible machine appliqué method.

Fresh Tip

If you have excess fabric on an outer point, trim it after you have starched and pressed down both sides of the point. If you ever press more fabric than you need, simply reapply starch to the portion that you need to re-press.

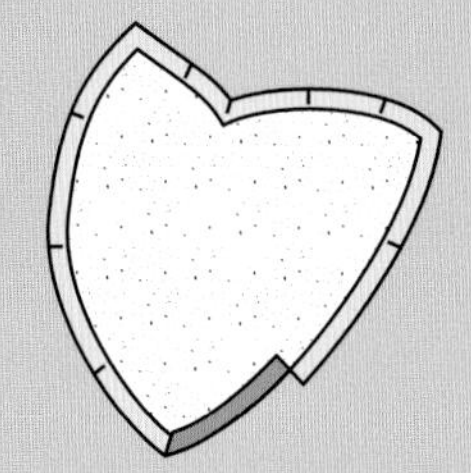

When working with an inner point, use the tip of your iron to press down one side and sweep the fabric in and over to the next side. Handle inner points as little as possible, but if necessary, take the tip of your iron and press directly into the point to secure the point and any stray threads.

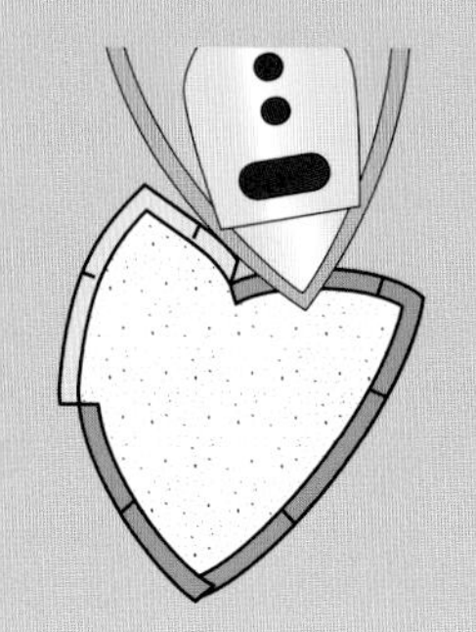

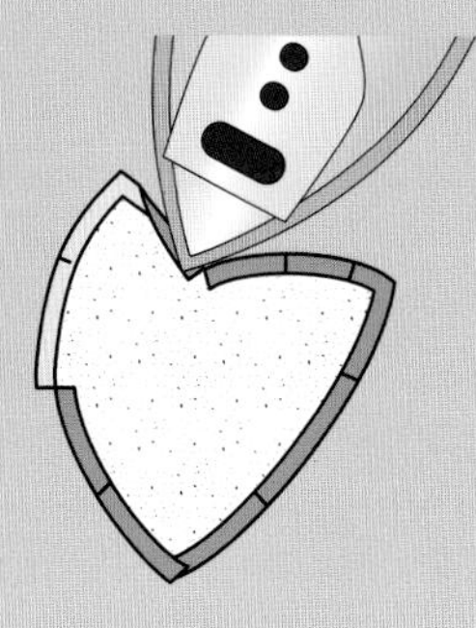

Traditional Appliqué Stitch

I exclusively use YLI 100-weight silk thread for hand appliqué. It comes in an array of colors, and because the thread is so thin it literally disappears into my fabric, even if my stitch is a little less than perfect.

To make the stitch, hold the turned-under portion of the appliqué firmly between your thumb and index finger. Bring the needle up through the background (the knot will be on the back of your fabric), and then through one or two threads of the turned edge of your appliqué shape. Insert the needle straight down into the *background fabric only*, straight across from where your needle came up. To take the next stitch, bring the needle up through the background, and then into the appliqué piece, approximately ⅛" from the last stitch. Take two stitches on inside and outside points. Continue in this way around the appliqué, finishing with a knot on the wrong side of the piece.

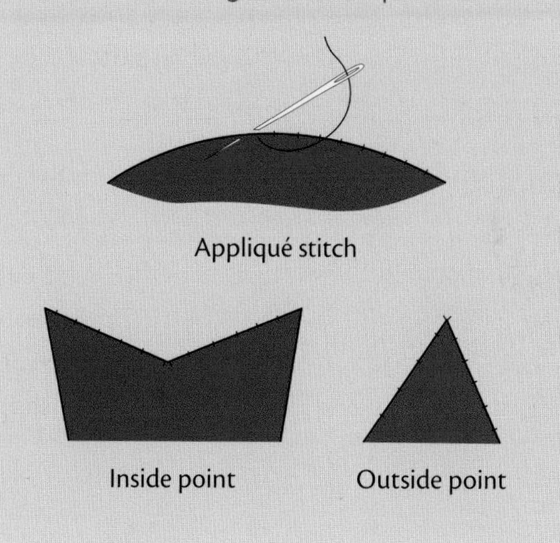

Wool Appliqué

Personally, when it comes to appliqué, I love to mix other fabrics with wool as often as I can. There is something unique about the pairing of cotton and wool that gives your projects a certain charm. My attraction for using wool is twofold. First, I love working with wool because of the texture and depth that it creates in a quilt. There is nothing like the interplay of cotton and wool to bring out the colors and the shapes of the appliqué. Second, and no less important, is that raw edges of felted wool can be left raw; wool does not have to be turned under because it doesn't fray. This makes it a wonderful medium to use for small, intricate pieces that you might not want to tackle if you were using a fabric that needed turning.

As much as I enjoy the addition of wool to my quilts, if you'd rather use cotton for any pieces that you have been instructed to cut from wool, just be sure to add seam allowance. Here are some additional tips you may find useful when working with wool:

- You can clip any stray threads after you cut the shape or after you appliqué, if necessary.
- The best stitch to use is a small, even whipstitch, but some people prefer to use a small blanket stitch (both have a similar effect visually), taking care to go in far enough to catch a sufficient portion of the wool. The blanket stitch can be done by hand or machine. See page 28 for instructions on how to make these stitches.
- Use YLI silk thread in a neutral tone–the thread completely disappears into the fabric. For a more primitive look, use a single strand of DMC floss or another thicker thread.
- Stitch carefully around outside points, taking stitches that are closer together at the point to define it.
- Overlap a couple of stitches at the end for strength.

FRESH TIP

When cutting out an intricate or detailed appliqué from wool, like the words on the photo album or dream journal, cut the freezer paper out at the same time you cut the wool. Just cut the template out in a large rectangle. Press the word template onto your wool piece, and then with small scissors cut through both the paper and the wool at the same time. This will make the process of cutting such small details much easier.

ADDING BORDERS

I recognize that borders are an area of much consternation for many quilters. I have even had students tell me that they have a closet full of quilt tops finished except for the borders. Many people hate choosing them. Many people hate measuring them. Many people hate sewing them on. Whatever your particular border problem happens to be, I hope that what follows might help you get those quilts out of the closet and onto the bed.

Style

I like to think of borders as a large frame for my quilt, or if there are several borders, a large mat, like the kind you might add to a painting or photograph. Sometimes you want that mat to be mellow and understated, simply there to bring out what is already in the painting. Other times you want that mat to be a vibrant part of the overall design, something that really brings the whole design together or completely changes the flavor or the feel of the entire piece. Whichever type of border or border grouping you are going for, follow these tips:

- Never choose a border until your quilt is done and you can hold it up or pin it up on a design wall and take a long, hard look at what it needs. Of course the second I make a rule, I want to break it. There have been times when my border fabric has been the entire inspiration for the quilt design, and, in those instances, I have broken my own rules and worked backward in terms of color and fabric selection. But usually the border is something that should not be decided until the quilt is at the "border stage" of design.
- The size of the border should be tied to the design elements of the interior of your quilt. A general guideline is that the first border shouldn't be any wider than either a dominant portion of the quilt block or the quilt center sashing, if there is sashing. If you're adding multiple borders, your eye often wants to see a smaller inner border that helps to close up and set off your pieced center. Again, this border should usually be somehow related to the pieces of your block.

FRESH TIP

Audition not only many different fabrics but also the widths that correspond to the widths of dominant pieces in your blocks. Most likely one of those widths will be the right "frame" for your quilt top.

Measuring

I know that many of you let out deep sighs when it comes to measuring and deciding how to cut the borders for your quilt, and I recognize that shortcuts are very tempting here. However, from personal experience I can tell you that well-measured borders can be the key to a good presentation of your quilt top. To achieve a successful, flat quilt without wavy borders or a bulging middle, you need to measure your quilt top carefully. The quilt instructions in this book usually don't give border measurements because it's too tempting for many people to just use the measurements provided instead of figuring their own.

When you're measuring your quilt for borders, take each measurement *two* times (more if your measurements are coming out different each time) to ensure that you have the correct length. For borders, it really is better to be safe than sorry. Cutting a border too short because of inaccurate measuring is a very frustrating mistake, especially if it means you have run out of fabric!

To measure your quilt top, measure through the vertical center and through the two vertical sides. If the measurements are different from one another, take the average of the three measurements and cut two borders to that length. Many times in order to have the length necessary, you will need to piece border strips together and then trim them to the exact length. Repeat this process for the top and bottom borders after you have stitched the side borders in place.

Sewing

Before you sew the borders to the quilt top, fold them in half crosswise to find the center. Do the same with the quilt top. With the centers and ends aligned, pin the borders to the quilt top at these points. Add more pins, easing the border in or out as necessary between the center and end pins and distributing the fabric evenly across the quilt top. Sew the borders in place. Press the seam allowances toward the borders. Repeat the process for the top and bottom borders.

FINISHING TECHNIQUES

Once your borders are stitched in place, don't be tempted to put your quilt back in the closet. Finish it up with quilting and binding so you can show it off. Instructions are provided here for selecting batting, layering the quilt in preparation for quilting, and binding the edges.

Selecting Batting

Many people ask what type of batting I use to get the soft drape and antique look. I have a couple of favorite battings that I seem to return to time and time again. The common thread between them is that they are thin, medium-loft, 100%-cotton battings.

Layering and Quilting

The backing, batting, and quilt top are layered to make the quilt sandwich. The layers are then temporarily basted together so they don't shift during the quilting process. The batting and backing should be cut at least 3" larger than the quilt top on all sides. For the quilts in this book, it will be necessary to sew two or three lengths of fabric together to make a backing the required size. Trim away the selvages before sewing the lengths together; press the seam allowance open. If your quilt design is elaborate or needs to be marked, do this before assembling the layers.

1. Place the backing, wrong side up, on a flat surface. Smooth out any wrinkles and secure it to the surface with masking tape at the corners. The backing should be taut but not stretched.

2. Spread the batting over the backing and smooth out any folds.
3. Center the pressed quilt top over the batting and smooth out any wrinkles. The quilt-top edges should be parallel to the edges of the backing.
4. For machine quilting, use size 1 rustproof safety pins to pin the layers together. Begin pinning in the center, working toward the outside edges and placing pins every 4" or so. For hand quilting, use a long needle and white thread to baste the layers together. Baste diagonally from corner to corner first, and then baste vertically and horizontally at 4" intervals. Baste around the quilt top edge using ¼" seam allowance.

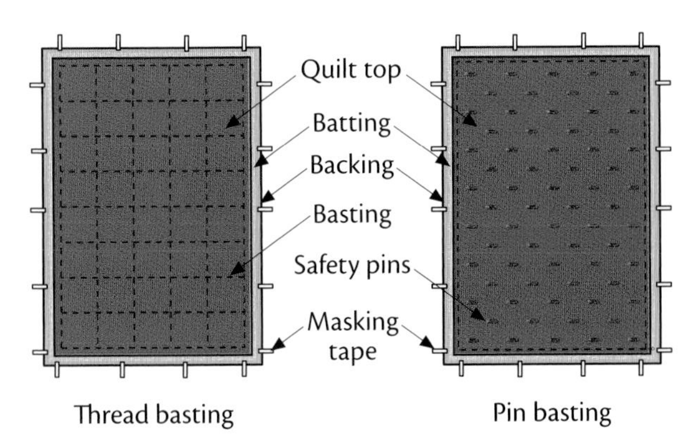

5. Hand or machine quilt the layers together. If you're machine quilting, remove pins as you go. Remove thread basting when you've finished hand quilting.
6. Trim the backing and batting ¼" beyond the quilt-top edges.

BINDING

I like to use double-fold binding for all my quilts. I cut the binding strips 2¼" wide, cutting across the width of the fabric. This allows just enough fabric to cover the sewing lines. Each project will specify the number of binding strips needed. You will have enough to cover the perimeter of the quilt plus approximately 18" for joining strips and mitering corners.

1. With right sides together, join the binding strips at right angles as shown to make one long strip. Trim the seam allowances to ¼" and press them open.

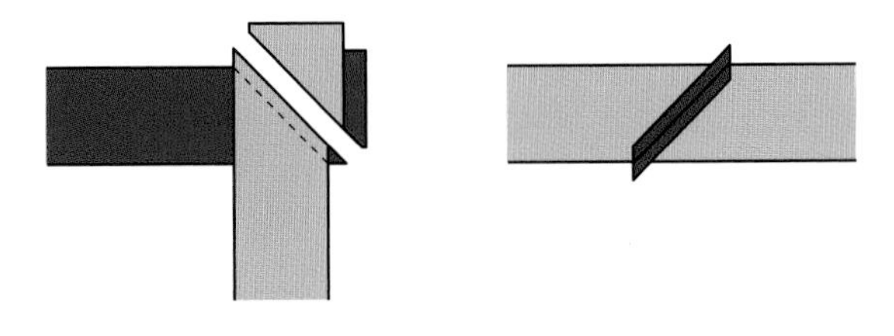

2. Press the strip in half lengthwise, wrong sides together.
3. Stitch the binding to the right side of the quilt through all the layers using a ¼" seam allowance. Start at the center of the bottom edge, leaving a tail approximately 9" long. Stop stitching ¼" from the first corner; backstitch and clip the threads. Remove the quilt from the machine.

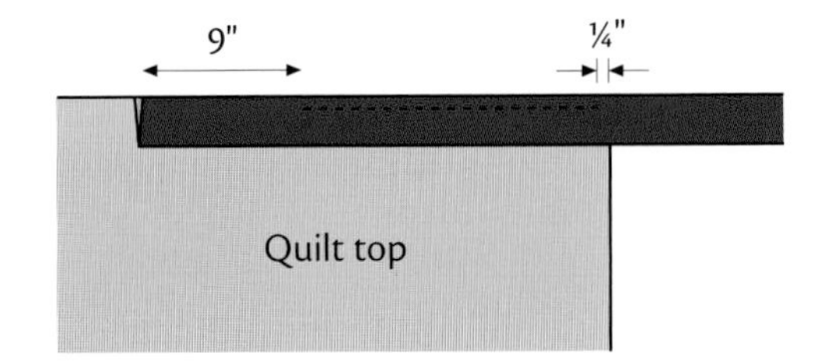

4. Turn the quilt so you're ready to sew the next side. Fold the binding strip up at a 90° angle so that the fold make a 45° angle, and then fold it back down on itself so the binding raw edge is even with the quilt raw edge. This will create a mitered corner. Stitch from the fold of the binding along the second edge of the quilt top, stopping ¼" from the next corner; backstitch. Continue stitching, repeating the mitering process on the remaining corners of the quilt.

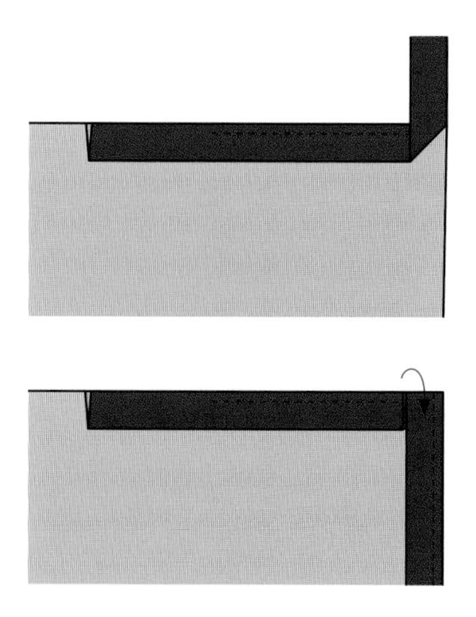

5. When you're approximately 12" from where you began stitching, backstitch and clip the threads. Overlap the binding ends 2¼" or the width of your binding strip; trim the excess. Open up the binding and place the ends at right angles to each other as shown, right sides together. Pin the ends in place, and then stitch diagonally from the upper-left corner of the top strip to where it meets the lower-right corner of the bottom strip. Open up your binding to make sure you sewed it correctly and that it fits the quilt top. Trim the seam allowance to ¼" and finger-press the seam allowance open.

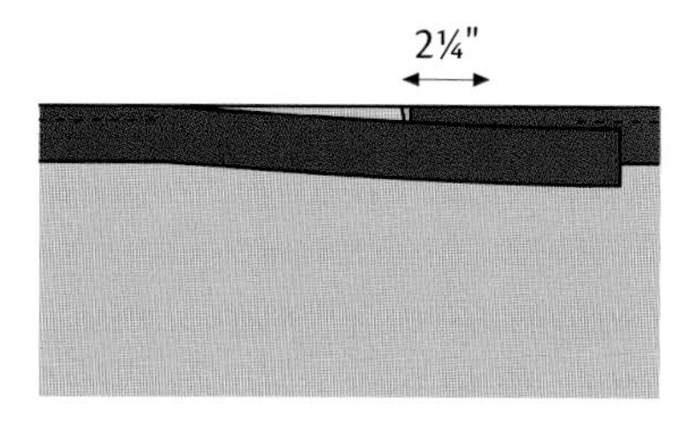

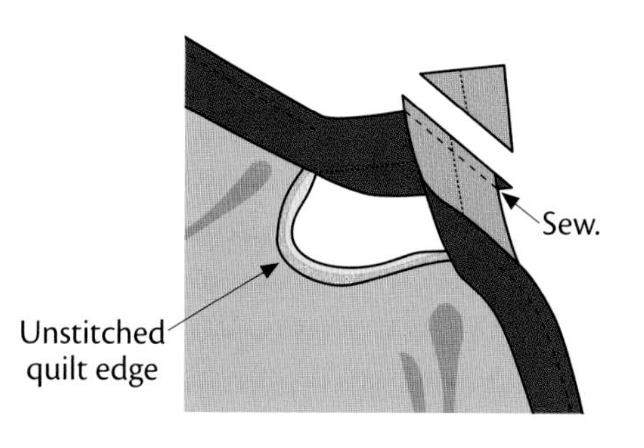

Fresh Tip

When you overlap the binding ends, pull them fairly tightly along the quilt. Remember that if you measure them "loosely," you most likely will have too much fabric in your binding and it will tend to ripple.

6. Sew the remainder of the binding to the quilt.
7. Turn the binding to the back of the quilt and hand blindstitch it in place, mitering the corners.

basic pincushion instructions

Jackie Cate has designed a wonderful array of three-dimensional projects for the ensembles in this book. While they are described as pincushions, they can be used as decorative elements in any room—with or without the pins, of course. All of the pincushions are constructed in basically the same way, so refer to the steps here for general step-by-step instructions and tips and to the project for specifics. Seam allowances have already been added to the patterns.

GENERAL SUPPLIES

Listed here are the supplies you'll need to have on hand for making any of the pincushions. Supplies needed in addition to those listed will be given in the materials section for each specific pincushion.

- Freezer paper
- Pencil
- Iron
- Scissors (paper, fabric, and small embroidery)
- Hemostat
- Crushed walnut hulls
- Cotton stuffing
- Funnel
- Hand-sewing needle

CUTTING AND ASSEMBLING THE PIECES

1. Trace each pattern given for the desired pincushion onto the dull side of a piece of freezer paper the number of times indicated. Cut each shape out on the drawn line.
2. Iron each freezer-paper shape, shiny side down, onto the wrong side of the appropriate fabric. Cut out each fabric shape, or trace around the freezer paper with your desired marking tool, remove the freezer paper, and then cut out the shape on the marked line.
3. With right sides together, stitch the pieces together as indicated in the project instructions, leaving an opening where indicated for turning. Backstitch at the beginning and end of each seam. Sew from the bottom to the top of the piece unless otherwise indicated.
4. Turn each piece right side out using a hemostat to grip the fabric and pull it through the opening. This nifty tool looks like a pair of scissors but is actually a locking clamp. You can find these at many quilt shops, medical-supply stores, and online. Gently run the closed hemostat along the seams inside the piece to smooth them out and shape the piece.

FRESH TIP

Feel free to mix and match fabrics for your pincushions. Wools, velvets, and cottons all work together beautifully. If you use velvet or very thin cotton, back the fabric with a lightweight fusible interfacing for stability and to reduce fraying.

Stuffing

Jackie uses crushed walnut hulls for the majority of the pincushion stuffing. Pet shops usually carry walnut hulls as litter for birds or lizards. A plastic funnel is useful when working with the hulls. She also uses a cotton stuffing called Sweet Dreams to help round out the pincushions. If you've left an opening for inserting a stem, put a small amount of cotton stuffing at the opening first so the hulls don't fall out.

1. After you've turned each piece, place the tip of the funnel into the opening and pour the walnut hulls into the funnel. As you go, shake the funnel so the hulls go down into the piece. At times you may need to remove the funnel and work the hulls down into the piece with your hemostat or by manipulating them with your hands. The trick is, when you think it's stuffed enough, keep going!
2. When you have plenty of walnut hulls in your piece, use the cotton stuffing to round out your pincushion. Grab a small piece of cotton stuffing with your hemostat and place the stuffing in the piece exactly where you need it. Once you've stuffed your piece to perfection, whipstitch the opening closed, unless otherwise indicated in the project instructions.

Stems

You have two options for stems. The first is to use a small branch from a tree, cut down to a size you think would look nice in your pincushion. Or, you can make your own stem from a piece of wool fabric. Cut the fabric 2" wide by the desired stem height, and then roll it tightly into a cylinder (you can run thin lines of glue along the inside of the fabric as you roll it to keep the piece intact). Once it's rolled as tightly as you'd like, whipstitch the raw edge down, going over it twice.

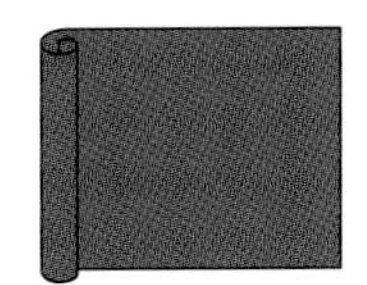
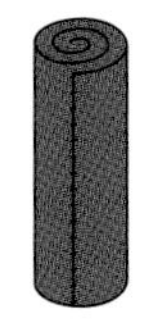

Insert the stem into the designated opening. Make sure the seam allowance around the opening is turned under. Stitch a running stitch around the opening, leaving a thread tail approximately 3" long at the beginning and end. Pull the thread tails to gather the fabric around the stem and close the opening; knot the ends twice and cut off the excess thread.

Beading

Adding beads to your pincushion is optional, depending on the look you want to achieve. Most of the pieces shown have beads added along the seam lines, with the exception of the carrot, which is beaded to imitate the horizontal lines of a real carrot.

1. Thread a thin needle (a size 11 straw works best) with one strand of coordinating floss or all-purpose thread and knot one end.
2. Push the needle into the pincushion so that the needle comes out at either the top or bottom of one of the seams. Gently pull on the thread until the knot pops into the inside of the pincushion. Clip any tail of thread that may not have been pulled inside with the knot.
3. Place a bead on the needle. Insert the needle back into the seam at or about the same point where you brought it out, and bring it out through the seam at the next place where you want to add a bead. Place the beads as close together or as far apart as you'd like. You can measure how far apart you'd like your beads prior to this step and mark those spots, but it's easy to estimate the distance while you are beading.

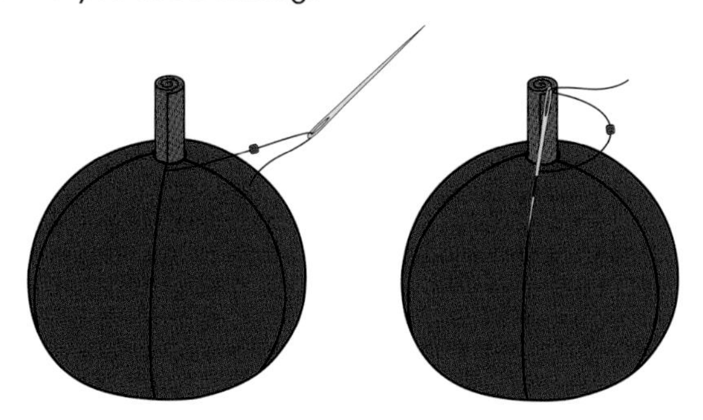

4. Add the desired amount of beads to the remainder of the seam. After you have added the last bead, knot the thread close to the pincushion, insert the needle into the piece and bring it out at another location. Pull on the thread to pop the knot inside the pincushion, and then clip the thread tail close to the piece.
5. Continue adding beads to the remaining seams in the same manner.

Leaves

Some of the fruit and vegetable pincushions will benefit from the addition of a leaf or two. Use felted wool so you don't have to finish the edges.

1. Use the leaf pattern given with the project to make a template as instructed in "Cutting and Assembling the Pieces" on page 25. Cut two pieces from felted wool for each leaf desired.
2. Place the two pieces together and whipstitch or blanket stitch (see page 28) around the edges with one strand of matching floss or all-purpose thread.
3. Whipstitch the stem end of the leaf to the pincushion near the stem.

Wired Leaves

If you want to be able to shape the leaf, cut a piece of green florist wire slightly shorter than the length of the leaf. Glue it through the lengthwise center of one of the leaves, leaving part of the stem end without wire so it can be stitched to the pincushion. With the wire on the inside, stitch the two leaf pieces together as described above.

special techniques

This section takes you through a variety of techniques that are used frequently throughout this book. Look here if you need instructions for making bias strips using a bias-tape maker, working a variety of embroidery stitches, or adding a flange.

CUTTING BIAS STRIPS

Strips cut on the fabric bias are more flexible than those cut on the straight grain, and they are absolutely necessary if you want to bind a curved edge or create curving vines. Bias strips are also a wonderful option if you simply like the way the strips look when cut at a 45° angle. Some people avoid bias strips because they believe that cutting them is complicated. Hopefully this method will put those fears to rest.

The instructions in this book will specify the total length of strips needed for your project. For future reference, to determine binding amounts, measure the perimeter of the project and add 18". For most projects, ½ yard of fabric will be sufficient, but you will be able to cut longer strips and do less piecing if you start with ⅝ or ¾ yard of fabric.

1. Open up your fabric and lay it on a flat surface so that the selvages are along the sides. Fold up the bottom edge so that the right-hand selvage is aligned with the top cut edge.

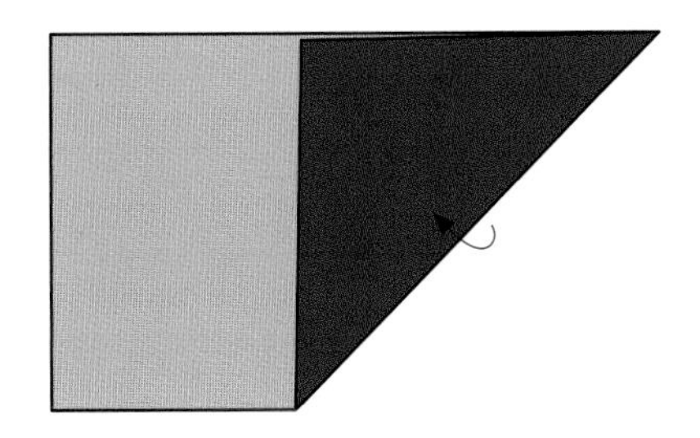

2. Fold the diagonal edge in half so the folded edges and points are aligned.

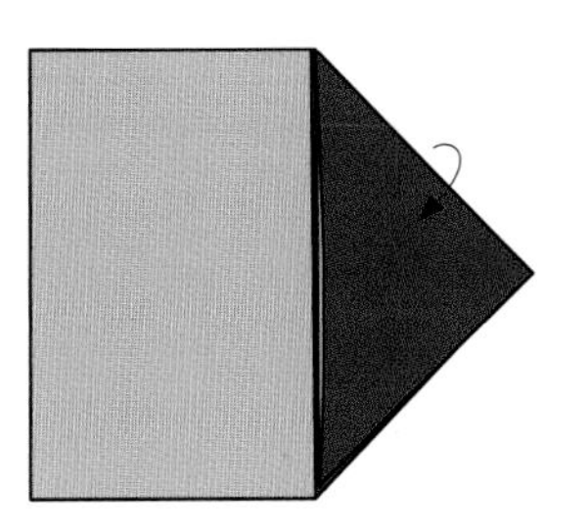

3. Barely trim off the lower folded edges.

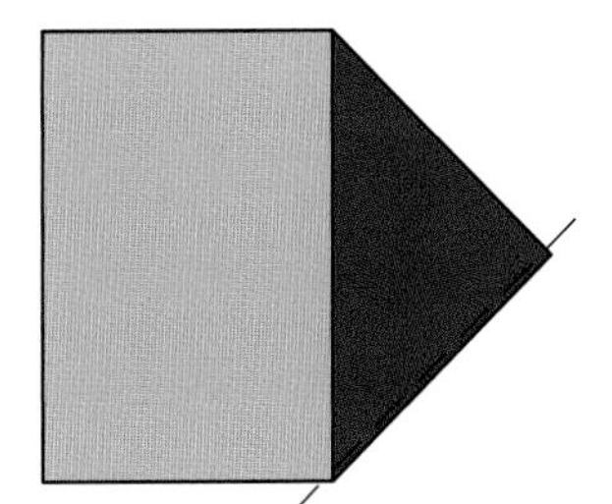

Trim folded edges.

4. Measuring from the trimmed edge, cut strips the width specified in the project instructions. For binding, cut strips 2¼" wide, cutting as many strips as needed to achieve the required length when they are pieced together.

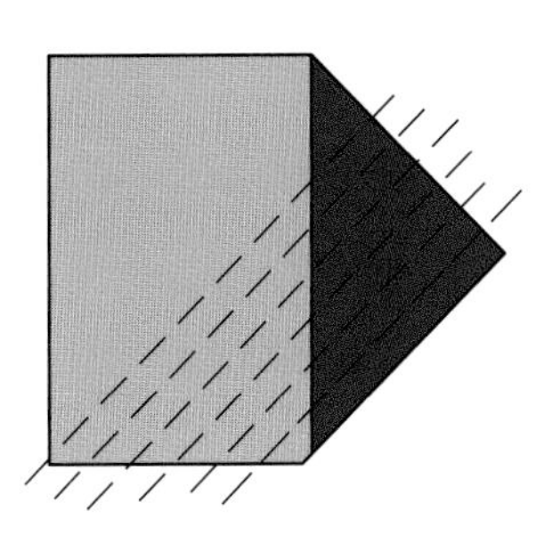

5. If you need to sew the strips together to achieve a long length, such as for binding, sew with right sides together, offsetting the seams ¼". Press the seam allowances open.

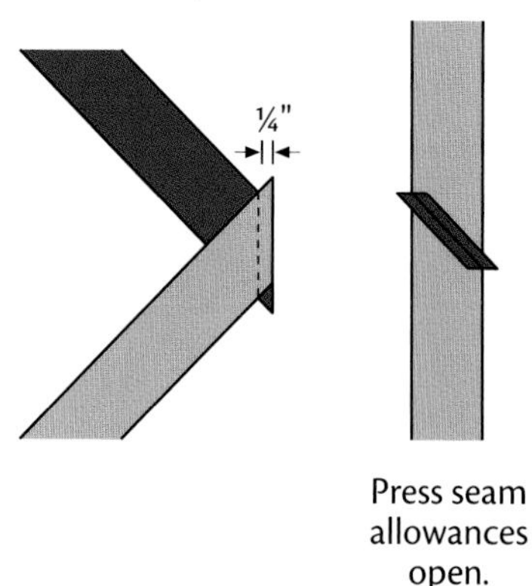

Press seam allowances open.

MAKING BIAS TAPE

I don't know how many of you have discovered bias-tape makers, but I think they are really wonderful, especially for making vines! They make the bias-tape process very simple and quick—better than anything else I've ever tried.

All bias-tape makers include instructions in the package, but here are some basic guidelines.

1. Cut your strip the desired width or the width indicated in the pattern instructions (it is usually twice the size of the finished width minus ⅛"). Personally, I like to cut them double the finished width because I feel that it makes the tape easier to work with and less likely to open up. If you have multiple strips, join them to make one long strip *only* if you absolutely need it for length. It is much easier to work with shorter pieces and hide the places where they join under other pieces.
2. Use a straight pin to pull one end of the strip through the tape maker, wrong side up. Center it inside the tape maker.
3. Place your iron on the end of the strip and perpendicular to it, and slowly begin to pull the tape maker away from the iron. Press the folds as they emerge from the tape maker. Keep even pressure on your iron as you go. When you have pulled the entire length through the tape maker, you will have a piece of bias tape ready for appliquéing.

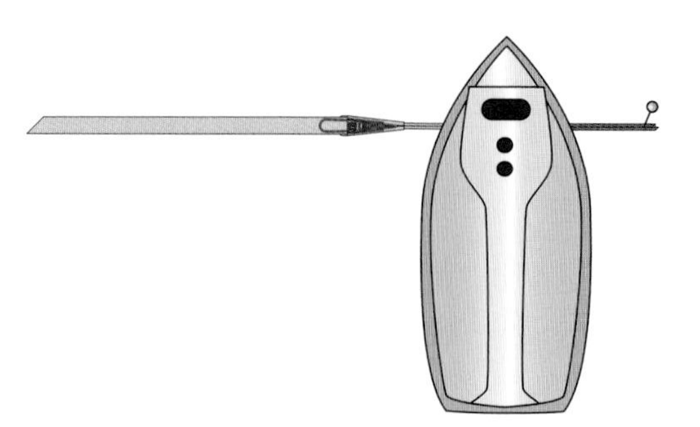

EMBELLISHING WITH EMBROIDERY STITCHES

Many of the sculpted fruits, vegetables, and other shapes are embellished with basic embroidery stitches. Some of these stitches are also used for wool appliqué. You don't need to be an embroidery expert to try them, and they really can add a wonderful touch to all kinds of projects.

Use size 5 pearl cotton or three strands of embroidery floss, unless otherwise indicated, and a size 5 embroidery needle. When you are finished making the stitches, bring the needle to the back and knot the thread or knot the thread first and bring it inside the work.

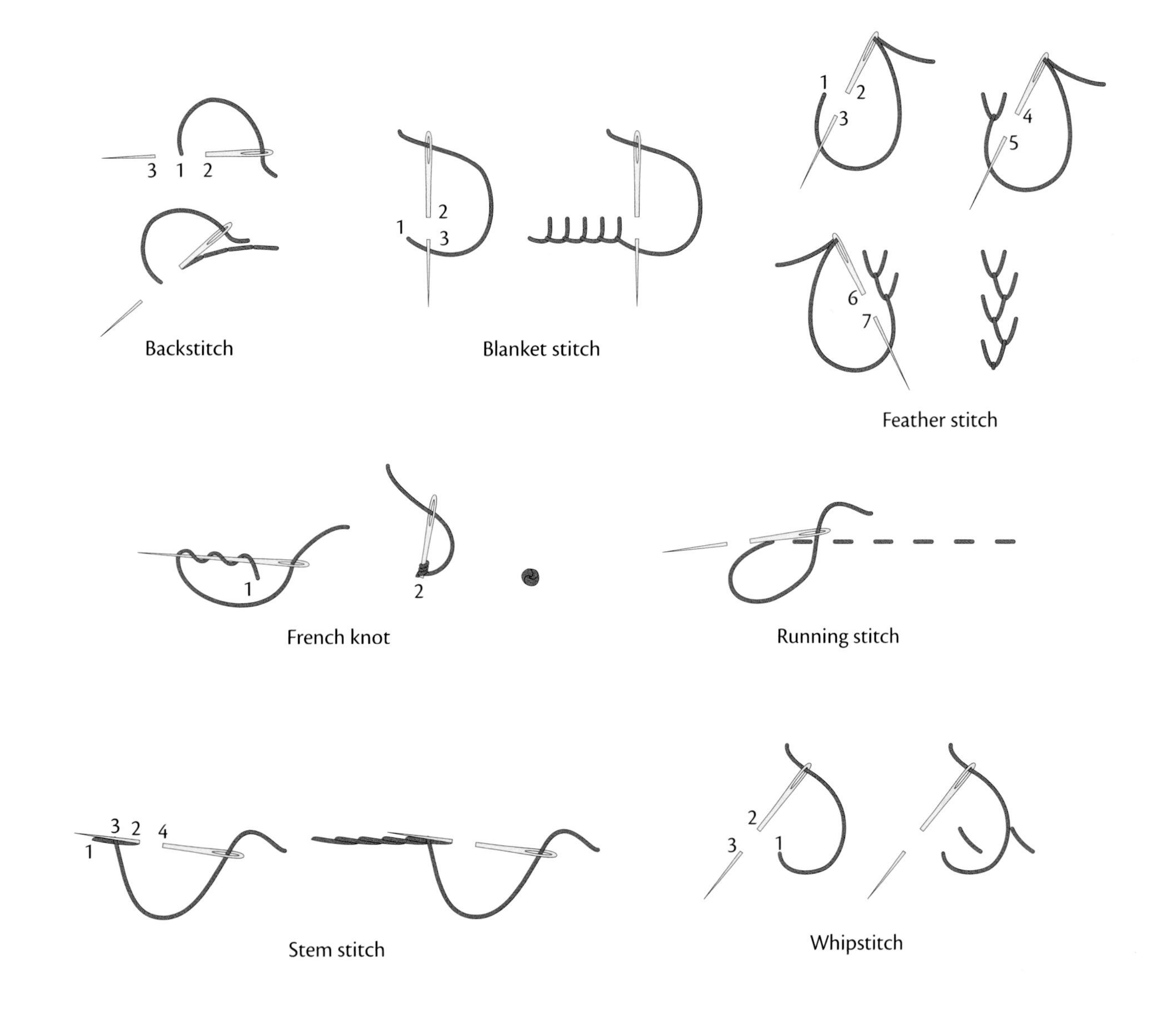

Backstitch

Blanket stitch

Feather stitch

French knot

Running stitch

Stem stitch

Whipstitch

ADDING A FLANGE

A flange is a folded fabric strip inserted into a seam that creates a trim detail. It is sometimes called flat piping because it is like piping without the cording inside to give it dimension. It can be made in various widths, depending on the look you want. The projects in this book use a ¼" finished flange, which the cut strip width in these instructions reflect. If you prefer a wider strip, just cut your strips wider; the instructions for making and applying the trim are the same.

1. Cut 1"-wide strips from your flange fabric, cutting across the width of the fabric. You will need one strip for each edge to which you will be applying the detail. The project instructions will specify this length.
2. Press each strip in half lengthwise, wrong sides together.
3. Position the strips on the right side of the project as instructed. Another layer of fabric will be added over the strips so that the strips are between two layers. Once the fabrics are stitched together, the flange detail will be created on the right side of the project.

Front Porch Welcome

This grouping makes me think of a spring morning in the country. I can literally hear the birds singing when I close my eyes. In my imagination there is a wraparound porch, an old porch swing with a quilt draped over it, and a beautiful table set with wonderful handmade goodies. I could spend all day there . . .

front porch blooms quilt

The idea for the block in this quilt began with a bird feeder! To be exact, it began with a picture of one of those wonderful bird feeders that has a giant sunflower head in the center, surrounded with layers of little dried flowers, bay leaves, and other yummy delights. The result was a wonderful porch decoration meant to entice the birds to come snack on the goodies. For me it meant the beginning of a quilt. I had long wanted to make one of those "sunburst" blocks, as I called them, but was not in the slightest bit interested in all of those templates. So after much mathematical manipulation, I figured out how to make a block that looks somewhat like one of those sunburst sunflowers without using a single template. This block is all strip pieced and straightforward to assemble. I have made them in both light spring versions and rich fall versions with equally pleasing results.

— Joanna

Finished quilt size: 63¼" x 63¼" Finished block size: 11" x 11"

MATERIALS

Yardages are based on 42"-wide fabrics.

¼ yard *each* of 16 assorted peach, spring green, aqua blue, butter yellow, and faded brown prints for blocks and sashing posts (see "Fabric Selection" below)

1⅛ yards of cream fabric for sashing

1⅛ yards of small-scale print for outer border

⅝ yard of fabric for binding

4 yards of fabric for backing

70" x 70" piece of batting

FABRIC SELECTION

You will need 16 different fabrics to make eight different pairs of fabric combinations. I recommend choosing a wide variety of colors and print sizes to give your stars visual interest. Make sure that you choose light, medium, and dark tones within your color palette so that the stars will stand out from one another and give your eyes a lot of variety to look at. Choose a lighter and a darker fabric for each block. From each duo you choose, you will be cutting enough pieces for two stars—one with the lighter fabric as the star and the darker fabric as the background and one vice versa. I recommend piecing the two blocks from each combination at the same time.

Designed by Joanna Figueroa;
pieced by Cheryl Hadley; quilted by Diana Johnson.

CUTTING

All measurements include ¼"-wide seam allowances. Before you cut the block fabrics, separate them into pairs as instructed in "Fabric Selection" and keep the cut pieces for each pair together.

From *each* of the 16 assorted print fabrics for blocks, cut:
1 strip, 7½" x 42"; crosscut the strip into:

- 1 piece, 7½" x 6½"; trim to 6½" x 6½" (A)
- 2 pieces, 7½" x 3¾"; crosscut *each* piece into 2 squares (4 total), 3¾" x 3¾". Cut each square twice diagonally to yield 16 triangles (B).
- 4 pieces, 7½" x 2¼"; trim each piece to 6¾" x 2¼". Crosscut *each* piece into 3 squares (12 total), 2¼" x 2¼" (C).
- 2 pieces, 7½" x 3"; trim each piece to 6" x 3". Crosscut *each* piece into 2 squares (4 total), 3" x 3" (D).
- 4 pieces, 7½" x 2¼"; trim each piece to 6" x 2¼". Crosscut *each* piece into 2 pieces (8 total), 2¼" x 3" (E).

From the leftover block fabrics, cut a *total* of:
25 squares, 2¾" x 2¾"

From the cream fabric, cut:
3 strips, 11½" x 42"; crosscut into 40 sashing pieces, 2¾" x 11½"

From the small-scale print, cut:
8 border strips, 4½" x 42"

From the fabric for binding, cut:
7 strips, 2¼" x 42"

PIECING THE BLOCKS

The instructions are for piecing two blocks at a time from one pair of fabrics.

1. Join one B triangle from each fabric to make a pair. Repeat with the remaining triangles from the two fabrics. Join two pairs to make an hourglass unit. Repeat to make a total of eight units. This will be enough for both blocks—they're identical to one another. Clip all the dog-ears.

Make 8.

HINT

Remember you aren't making half-square triangles, so sew along one of the *short* sides of the triangle when piecing.

2. Refer to "Triangle Units" on page 17 to join a C square to each corner of the A square from the other fabric, orienting and sewing on the fold lines as shown. Repeat to make one additional unit, reversing the fabric placement.

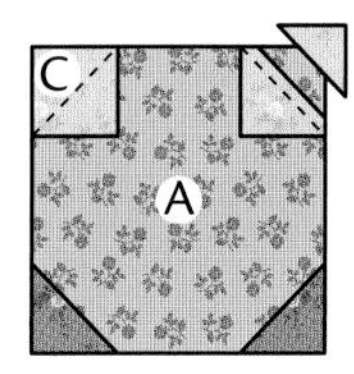

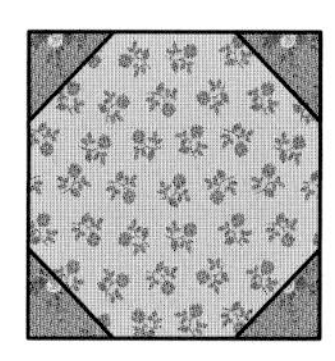
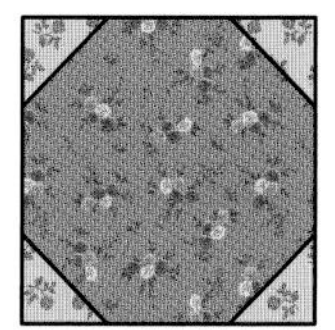

Make 1 of each.

3. Refer to "Triangle Units" to join a C square to eight E pieces from the other fabric, orienting and sewing four squares with the fold line in one direction and four squares with the fold line in the other direction as shown. Reverse the fabric placement and make eight additional units as shown.

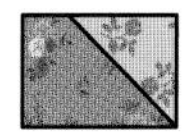

Make 4.

Make 4.

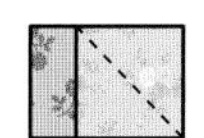

Make 4.

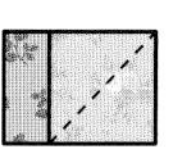
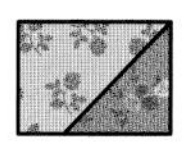

Make 4.

4. Arrange the units from steps 1–3 and the D squares into three vertical rows for each of the two blocks. Be sure the star points are the same fabric as the A square in each block and that they are oriented correctly. Sew the pieces in each row

together. Press the seam allowances as indicated. Sew the rows together. Press the seam allowances toward the outer rows.

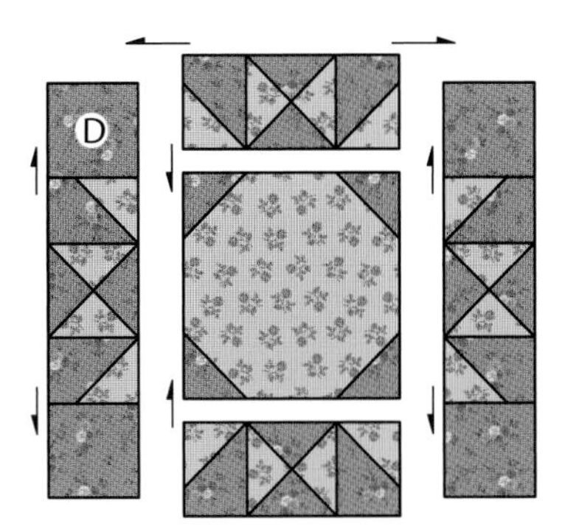

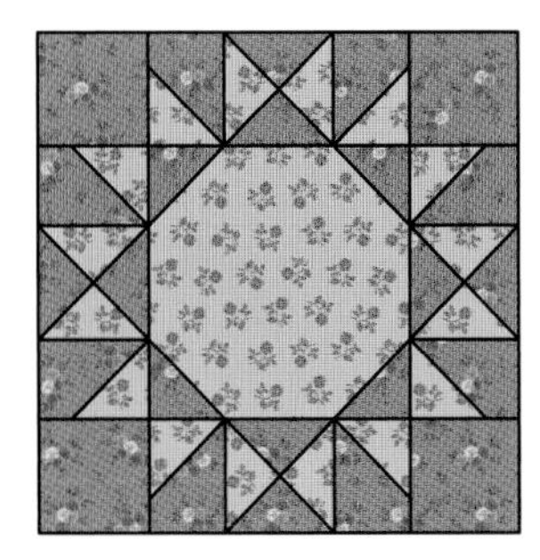

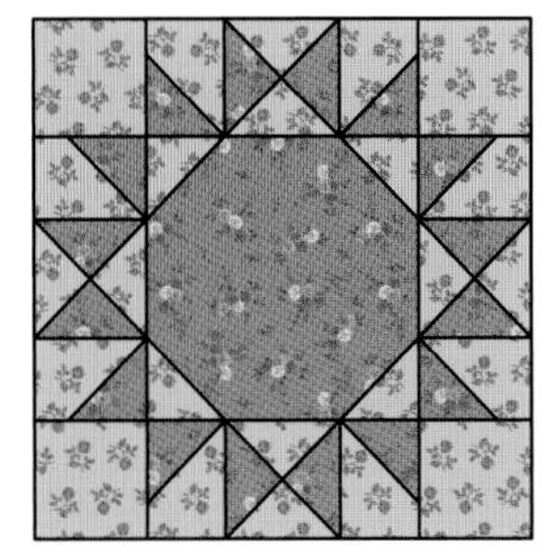

Make 1 of each.

FRESH TIP

Be sure you're sewing the correct pieces together. I recommend laying out each of the two blocks in each pair before you sew the pieces together to avoid confusion, at least for the first three or four duos that you piece.

ASSEMBLING THE QUILT TOP

1. To make the block rows, arrange the blocks in four rows of four blocks each, repositioning blocks as needed until you're satisfied with the arrangement. Be sure to notice the placement of the lighter and darker blocks to create a visual balance. Refer to the assembly diagram to place a sashing piece vertically between each block. Join the blocks and sashing pieces in each row. Press the seam allowances toward the sashing pieces.
2. To make the sashing rows, join four sashing pieces and five sashing post $2\frac{3}{4}$" squares as shown. Make five rows. Press the seam allowances toward the sashing pieces.

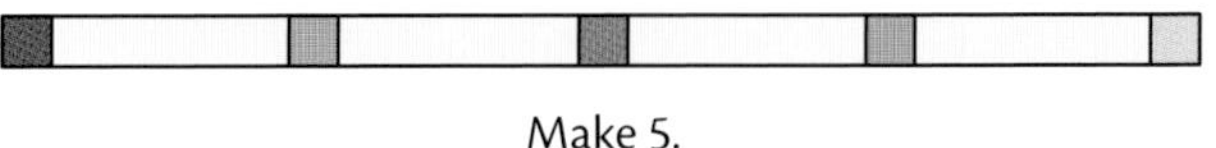

Make 5.

3. Sew the block rows and sashing rows together. Press the seam allowances toward the sashing rows.
4. Refer to "Adding Borders" on page 20 to add the small-scale print $4\frac{1}{2}$"-wide border strips to the quilt top, piecing the strips as necessary.

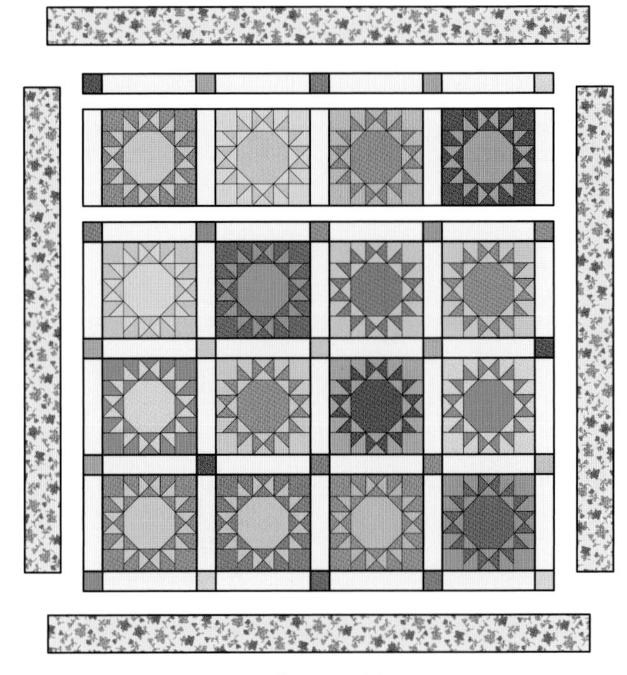

Quilt assembly

FINISHING THE QUILT

Refer to "Finishing Techniques" on page 21 for detailed instructions.

1. Layer the quilt top with batting and backing; baste.
2. Quilt as desired. Diana used some wonderful heirloom quilting designs on this quilt to reinforce the idea of the blooms as sunflowers. She crosshatched the block centers and created a beautiful feathered wreath design around the points. She continued the cross-hatching in the sashing posts and the feathers in the sashing pieces. The result is a wonderful, vintage-inspired heirloom quilt.
3. Bind the quilt edges with the $2\frac{1}{4}$"-wide binding strips.

sit awhile seat cushions

Designed and made by Janis Stob and Margaret Linderman.

While driving through the country, we found lots of great chairs lined up on wraparound porches, inviting us to come sit and take a break from a busy day. Upon arriving home we had to create that same type of setting for ourselves. Soft cushions made with delicate floral prints and stripes just say "home."

—Janis and Margaret

Finished cushion size: 17" x 17"

MATERIALS

Yardages are based on 42"-wide fabrics. Materials given are enough for 2 cushions.

4 fat quarters of coordinating prints for top outer pieces (one edge must be at least 20" long)

1 fat quarter of print for top centers

1⅔ yards of striped fabric for backs, bindings, and ties

1 yard of fusible batting or fusible fleece

2 squares, 18" x 18", of 1½"-thick foam*

Freezer paper

We have foam cut and covered with a polyester fabric at a local foam shop for extra softness. You can find uncovered foam at many chain fabric stores.

CUTTING

All measurements include ¼"-wide seam allowances.

From the fat quarter for the top centers, cut:
2 squares, 9½" x 9½"

From *each* of the 4 coordinating fat quarters, cut:
2 pieces, 5" x 14"

From the striped fabric, cut:
2 pieces, 8" x 18"

2 pieces, 17" x 18"

Set aside the remainder of the fabric for cutting bias strips.

From the fusible batting, cut:
2 squares, 18" x 18"

PIECING THE CUSHION COVER TOPS

1. Using four different coordinating 5" x 14" pieces, place one piece along the top of a 9½" square, right sides together with one side aligned. Sew the pieces together, stopping at the center of the square. Press the seam allowance away from the square. Sew another piece to the right side of the unit. Press the seam allowance away from the square. Add another strip to the bottom edge of the unit, and press the seam allowance away from the square. Sew the last strip to the lower-left side of the unit, keeping the first piece out of the way. Press the seam allowance away from the square. Sew the remaining portion of the first seam. Repeat step 1 to make a total of two cushion tops.

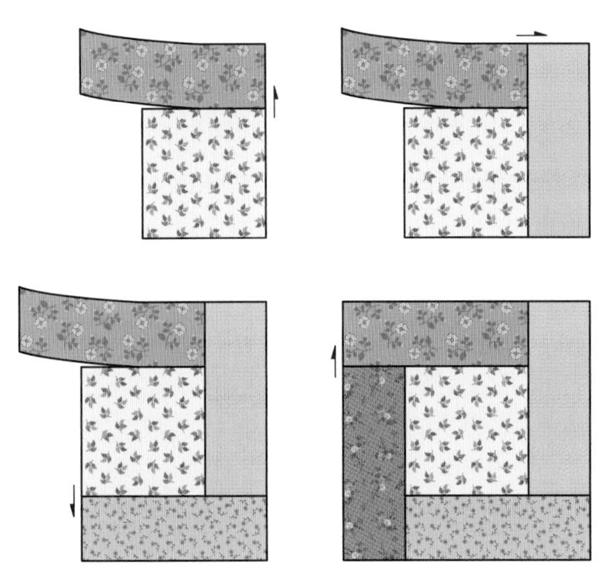

Make 2.

2. Follow the manufacturer's instructions to fuse a batting square to the wrong side of each top.
3. Stitch ¼" from the seam lines on each coordinating fat quarter piece.

ASSEMBLING THE CUSHION COVERS

1. On each 8" x 18" piece, press under 1" along the 18" edge, and then press under 1" again. Topstitch the hem in place. These are the upper-back pieces and should now measure 6" x 18". Repeat with the 17" x 18" pieces to make two lower-back pieces, each 15" x 18".
2. Lay an upper-back piece on your work surface, wrong side up with the hemmed edge closest to you. Place a lower-back piece over the upper-back piece, wrong side up, so that the hemmed edges of the two pieces overlap 3" and the raw edges of both pieces are along the outer edges. Position a cushion top over the back pieces, right side up, aligning the raw edges. Pin the layers together. Repeat with the remaining top and back pieces.

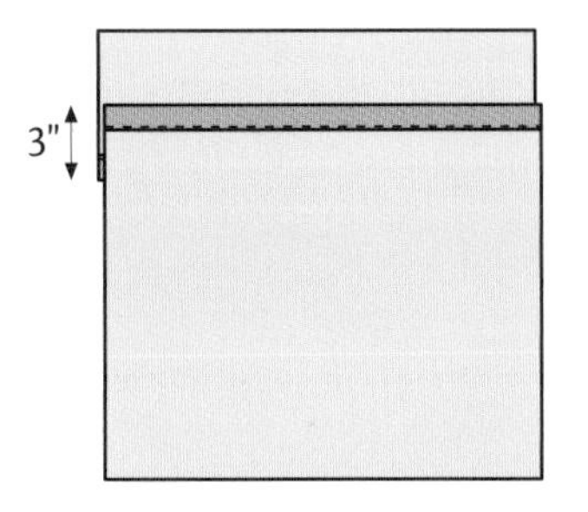

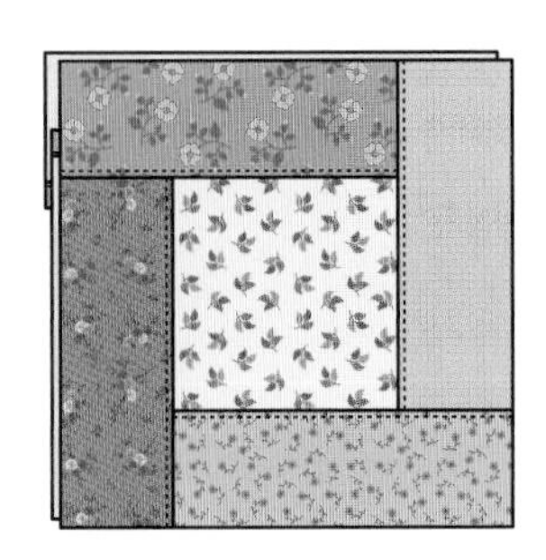

3. Use the corner trimming pattern on page 37 to make a template from freezer paper, and then use the template to trim the corners of each set of layered cushion-cover pieces.

FINISHING THE CUSHION COVERS

1. Refer to "Cutting Bias Strips" on page 27 to cut 2¼"-wide bias strips from the remaining striped fabric. You will need four strips, 20" long, for the edge ties; 12 strips, 12" long for the closure ties; and a strip for the binding that measures approximately 150" long when pieced together.
2. Refer to "Binding" on page 22 to bind the edges of each cushion cover with the binding strip. The process is the same as for a quilt, only you will not have a layer of batting between the top and back pieces.
3. To make the edge ties, press each 2¼" x 20" bias strip in half lengthwise, wrong sides together. Fold each strip into thirds lengthwise, folding the long raw

edge to the center first, and then folding the first folded edge over it. Topstitch along the first folded edge. Tie a knot at both ends of each strip.

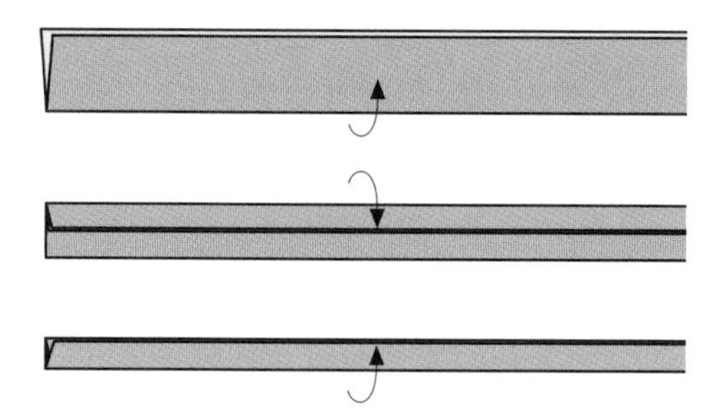

4. Repeat step 3 to make the closure ties, but knot only one end of each strip. Press under the unknotted end ½".
5. Fold each edge tie in half. Position the fold of a tie at the upper corners of each upper-back piece at the edge of the binding. Stitch through all layers. Place the pressed end of three closure ties along the hemmed edge of each upper-back piece, positioning one in the center and one at each end. Stitch the pressed end in place through the back piece only. Position the remaining ties on the lower-back pieces so they line up across from the upper-back ties and are approximately 2" from the lower-back edge. Stitch the pressed end in place through the back piece only.

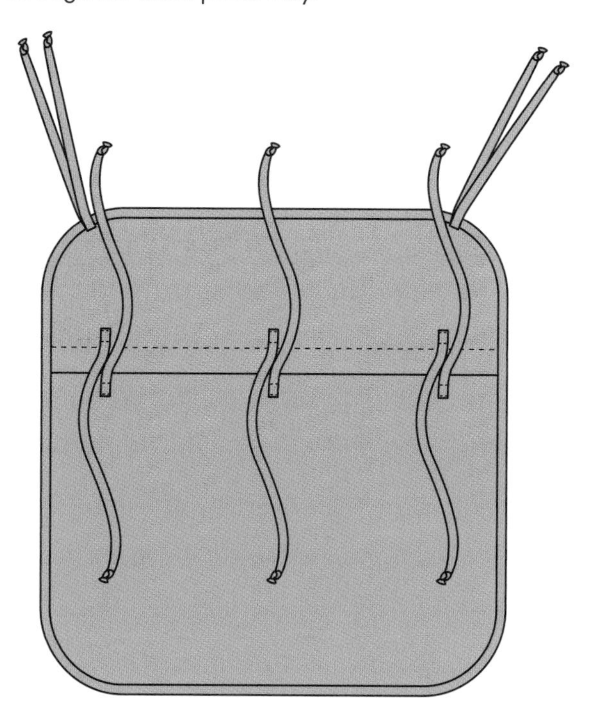

6. Insert a foam square into each cushion cover and tie the openings closed. Place each cushion on a chair with the edge ties toward the back. Tie the ties to the chair back or legs. Grab a book and have a seat!

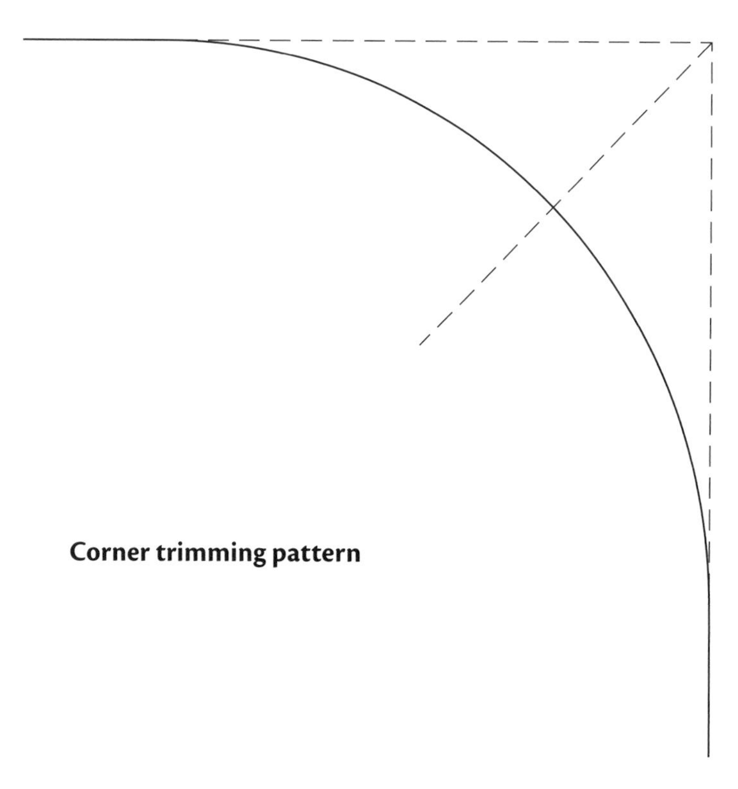

Corner trimming pattern

front porch guests

Designed and sewn by Jackie Cate.

Birds, birds, birds—I love birds! I love watching them and hearing them outside. I love bird pictures, bird postcards, little metal birds around my house—anything bird, I love! We have lots of birds in our yard, and every year they come and sing and build their nests in our trees and on our house. These little ones represent the little, chubby, happy birds I love to watch from my window while I sew.

—Jackie

MATERIALS

Amounts given are enough to make one bird and three large or small eggs. In addition to the materials given below, you will need the general pincushion supplies listed on page 24.

Bird

9" x 18" piece *total* of fabric scraps for body and head (you can use 1 or 2 different fabrics for the body and head)

4 squares, 4" x 4", of fabric for wings (you can use 1 fabric for the outside and 1 for the inside, or 1 fabric for both)

2 squares, 5" x 5", of fabric for tail (again, you can use 2 different fabrics)

2" x 2" square of coordinating felted wool for bottom

½" x ½" square of brown felted wool for beak

Doll-making needle

Size 5 black pearl cotton for eyes

Hand-quilting thread to match fabrics

8" of green florist wire

Tacky glue

Eggs

12 squares, 4" x 4", of assorted fabrics

Bird nest (3" to 4" diameter for small eggs, 6" diameter for large eggs)

MAKING THE BIRD

Refer to "Basic Pincushion Instructions" on page 24.

1. Use the patterns on page 41 to make freezer-paper templates for the bird head and body. Do not cut templates for the wing and tail yet. Cut out the pieces from the desired fabrics.
2. Place two body pieces right sides together. Sew along one curved edge, sewing from the straight edge to the point. Repeat to make one additional pair. Press the seam allowances in opposite

directions. With right sides together and seams matching, sew the pairs together along the curved edges. Start at one side of the straight edge and stitch around the curved edges to the other side of the straight edge, backstitching at the beginning and end.

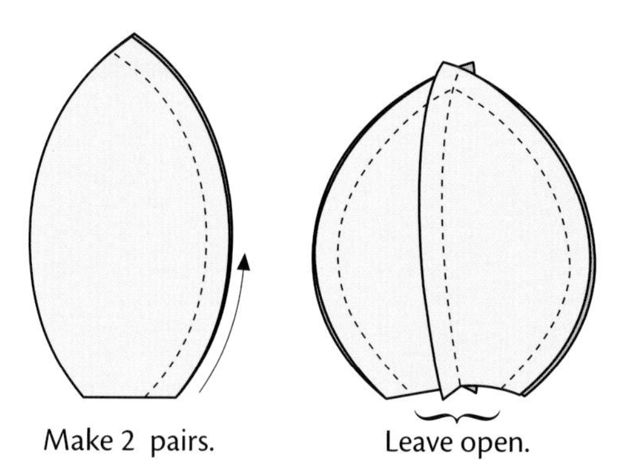

3. Turn the body right side out and stuff it with crushed walnut hulls and cotton batting. Stitch the opening closed.
4. For the head, sew the three pieces together side by side along the curved edges, right sides together. Again, sew from the bottom to the rounded end at the top. Bring the two unstitched curved edges on each side right sides together; sew. Make sure there isn't a gap at the rounded end, because this will be the front of the bird's face.

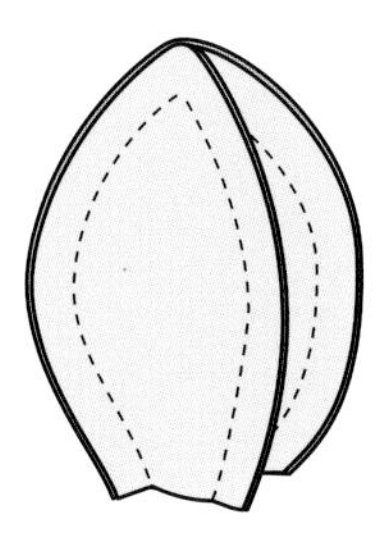

5. Turn the head right side out, stuff it, and then stitch the opening closed.
6. Decide which section will be the top of the head. Thread the doll-making needle with pearl cotton. Make a knot on one end. Insert the needle into the head from the back, and come out on one of the top side seams where you want to make an eye. Make a French knot. Pull the needle out at the same spot on the other top side seam and make another French knot. Pull the needle out through the back of the head and clip the thread.
7. Thread the doll-making needle with hand-quilting thread. Place the straight ends of the bird body and head together like you want them on the finished bird. Insert the needle into the front of the bird's head and out through one of the body seams. Pull the thread to bury the knot, take a tiny stitch in the seam, and then go back out through the front of the head. Repeat until the head is firmly attached to the body. Apply tacky glue between the head and the body for extra security. Let the glue dry.
8. Place the brown wool ½" square at the point on the bird's face where all the seams match and tack it in place with matching thread. This is the bird's beak.
9. Trace the wing and tail patterns onto freezer paper and cut them out.
10. For the wings, place two 4" squares of the wing fabric right sides together. If you want the top and the bottom of the wing to be different, make sure you are using one square from each fabric. Iron the freezer-paper template to the top fabric and trace around it with the desired marking tool. Remove the template. Sew on the marked line, making sure to leave the straight edge open as indicated. Cut out the piece ¼" from the stitching. Repeat with the remaining two wing squares.
11. Turn the wings right side out and use a hemostat, if necessary, to push out the seams and shape the wings; press. Stitch the opening on each wing closed.
12. Place a wing on the side of the bird body and whipstitch the front portion in place. I leave the back portion of the wing free, so that it sticks out a little bit and looks like the bird is ready to take off. Attach the remaining wing to the other side of the body.
13. For the tail, place the two 5" squares right sides together and iron the freezer-paper template to the top fabric; trace around it. Remove the paper and sew on the marked line, leaving the straight edge open. Cut out the piece ¼" from the stitching. Turn the tail right side out and push out the seams; press. Topstitch ⅛" from the stitched edges, leaving the straight edge open.

14. Cut the florist wire in half. Insert a piece of wire into the openings created along the left and right sides of the tail by the topstitching. Work the wire all the way to the top corner. Cut off any excess wire at the opening.
15. Pin the tail to the back of the bird. Cover the bottom of the tail with the 2" square of wool. If desired, you can cut the square into a circle. I've used both shapes, and also pinked the edges for added interest. Just make sure the final shape covers the bottom of the tail. Lightly glue the piece in place, and once the glue is dry, whipstitch around the edges.
16. Use your bird as is or find him a little nest to sit in!

MAKING THE EGG

Refer to "Basic Pincushion Instructions" on page 24. The instructions are the same for the small or large egg.

1. Use the pattern below to make freezer-paper templates for either the large or small egg. Cut out the pieces from the 4" squares of assorted fabrics.
2. Referring to step 2 of "Making the Bird," sew the pieces together in pairs, and then sew the two pairs together.
3. Turn the eggs right side out and stuff them with crushed walnut hulls and cotton batting. Stitch the openings closed.
4. Arrange the eggs in the nest and use either a hot glue gun or tacky glue to secure them to the bottom.

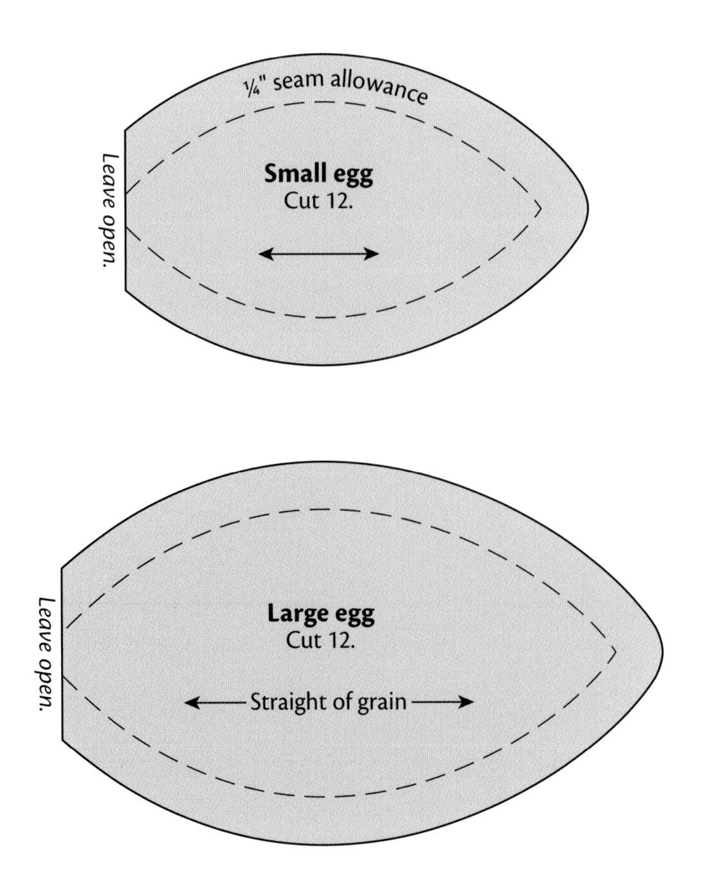

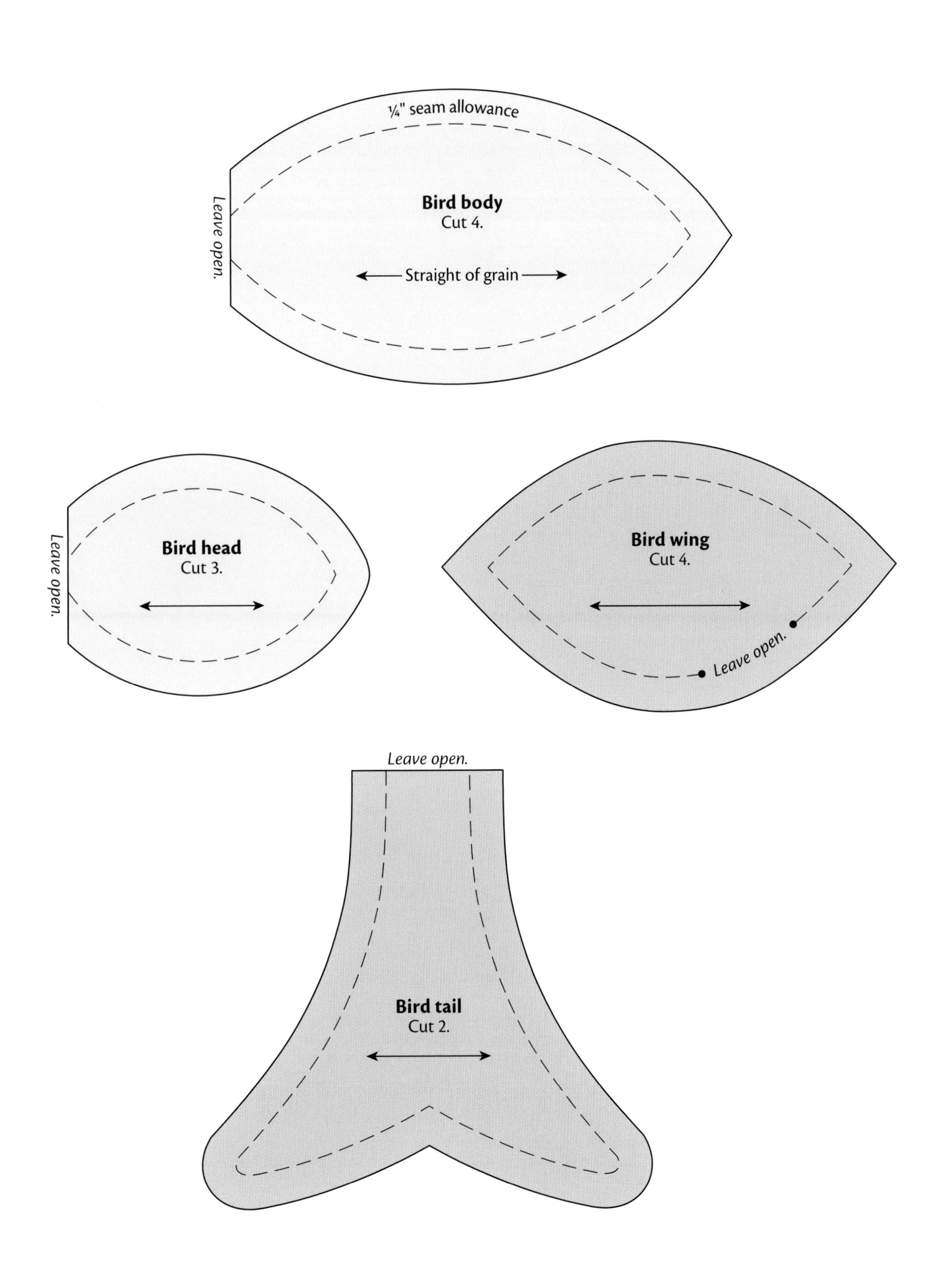
¼" seam allowance
Leave open.
Bird body
Cut 4.
Straight of grain
Leave open.
Bird head
Cut 3.
Bird wing
Cut 4.
Leave open.
Leave open.
Bird tail
Cut 2.

Harvest Medley

This grouping is autumnal and soft and vintage all at the same time. The quilt makes me think that fall is just around the corner and that the leaves will start falling any time. It's perfect for keeping your lap warm while you sip a cup of your favorite tea or coffee. The sweet and simple apron makes me want to whip up a batch of oatmeal raisin cookies. And the Harvest Table fruits . . . well could you think of a more perfect fall centerpiece?

harvest moon quilt

Harvest Moon started as a block exchange with the Morning Threads ladies, a weekly quilting group of which I am a member. The blocks from that exchange created the background for this fun, seasonal quilt. My sincere thanks to the group for giving me a start on this quilt, which will always remind me of the fun and laughter we share.

—Denise

Finished quilt size: 65½" x 65½" Finished block size: 14" x 14"

MATERIALS

Yardages are based on 42"-wide fabrics.

16 fat quarters of assorted light prints for blocks

16 fat quarters of assorted dark prints for blocks

1 yard of fabric for outer border

⅞ yard of green plaid for bias stems and small leaves

½ yard of fabric for inner border

2 squares, 10½" x 10½", of assorted cream prints for pumpkins

2 squares, 10½" x 10½", of assorted tan prints for pumpkin appliqués

2 pieces, 7" x 10", of assorted dark green prints for gourd appliqués

2 pieces, 7" x 10", of assorted light green prints for gourd appliqués

Scraps of assorted orange, peach, yellow, and terracotta prints for flower appliqués

Scraps of assorted green prints for leaf and calyx appliqués

Scraps of brown fabrics for pumpkin stem appliqués

½ yard of fabric for binding

4 yards of fabric for backing

72" x 72" piece of batting

Bias-tape maker

Designed by Denise Sheehan; sewn by Denise Sheehan and Morning Threads friends; quilted by Diana Johnson.

CUTTING

All measurements include 1/4"-wide seam allowances.

From *each* of the 16 fat quarters of assorted light prints, cut:

1 square (16 total), 10 3/8" x 10 3/8"

1 square (16 total), 8 1/2" x 8 1/2"; cut twice diagonally to yield 4 (64 total) triangles

From *each* of the 16 fat quarters of assorted dark prints, cut:

1 square (16 total), 8 1/2" x 8 1/2"; cut twice diagonally to yield 4 (64 total) triangles

From the fabric for inner border, cut:

8 strips, 1 3/4" x 42"

From the fabric for outer border, cut:

8 strips, 4" x 42"

From the fabric for binding, cut:

7 strips, 2 1/4" x 42"

PIECING THE BLOCKS

1. Stitch a light triangle and a dark triangle together to make a triangle unit. Repeat with the same fabrics to make four identical units. Press the seam allowances toward the dark triangles. Repeat with the remaining light and dark triangles to make 16 sets of four matching units.

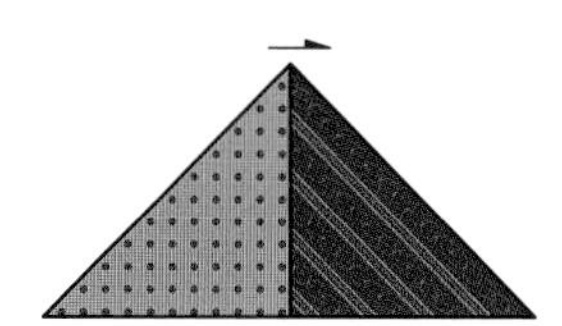

Make 16 sets of 4 matching units.

2. Fold a light square in half lengthwise and crosswise; finger-press to mark the center. Open up the square. Place a step 1 unit with a matching light triangle right sides together with the square, lining up the seam of the triangle unit with the fold along one side. Stitch the unit in place. Repeat with a

matching triangle unit on the opposite side of the square. Press the seam allowances toward the square. Repeat with the remaining two matching triangle units on the remaining sides of the square. Square up the block to 14½". Repeat to make a total of 16 blocks.

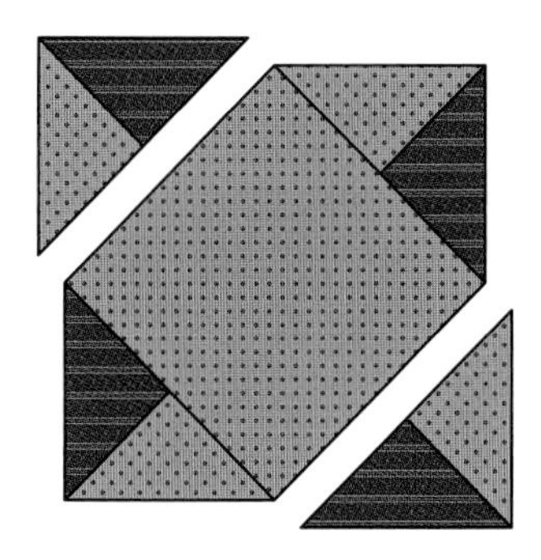

APPLIQUÉING THE BLOCKS

1. Refer to "Cutting Bias Strips" on page 27 to cut 1"-wide bias strips from the green plaid fabric. You will need seven lengths approximately 15" long. Piece strips together as necessary to achieve the desired length. Refer to "Making Bias Tape" on page 28 to make ½"-wide bias tape from the strips for the stems.
2. Refer to "Appliqué" on page 17 and use the patterns on pages 46–50 to prepare the appliqué shapes for each block. Use the photo at left and the materials list for fabric choices if needed.
3. Refer to the photo at left to appliqué the shapes for the desired motif to each block, working in numerical order. Use the bias tape you made in step 1 for the vines. For vines that cross into another block, leave the end that crosses into another block free. It will be appliquéd in place after the blocks are sewn together.

ASSEMBLING THE QUILT TOP

1. Arrange the blocks into four rows of four blocks each as desired or use the photo as a guide. Sew the blocks in each row together, making sure any loose vines are out of the seam line. Press the seam allowances in opposite directions from row to row. Sew the rows together, again making sure you don't catch any loose vines. Press the seam allowances in one direction.
2. Appliqué any loose vines in place.
3. Sew the 1¾" x 42" inner-border strips together in pairs and trim each pair to 1¾" x 71". Sew the 4" x 42" outer-border strips together in pairs and trim each pair to 4" x 71". Stitch each inner-border strip to an outer-border strip, right sides together.
4. Fold each joined border strip in half crosswise and mark the edge of the inner-border strip at the center with a pin. Fold the quilt top in half in each direction and mark the center of each edge with a pin. On the wrong side of the quilt top, mark a dot ¼" from each corner.
5. With right sides together and raw edges even, pin a border strip to one side of the quilt top, matching center points. Be sure the raw edge of the inner-border strip is aligned with the raw edge of the quilt. Start pinning at the center, and work your way to the edges. Your border will be longer than the quilt top. With the wrong side of the quilt top facing up, stitch the border in place, starting and stopping at the marked dots. Backstitch at the beginning and end of the seam. Press the seam allowance toward the border. Repeat with the remaining border strips on each side of the quilt.
6. Lay the first corner to be mitered on your ironing board. Lay the borders straight and flat, so that they overlap at the corners as shown.

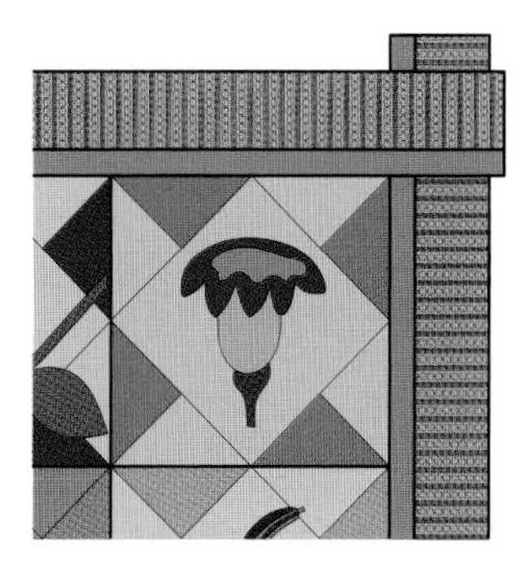

7. Fold the top-border strip under at a 45° angle, aligning the edges with the adjacent border strip. Press the fold with your iron. Use a square ruler with a 45° angle marking to check the accuracy of the fold. Carefully lift up the top border and place a piece of double-stick tape just inside the crease.

Lay the border back in place and check accuracy again using your ruler; adjust if necessary.

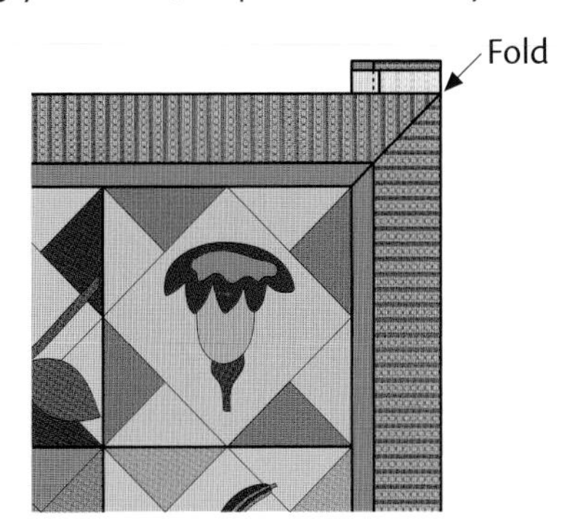

8. Carefully fold the quilt top in half diagonally right sides together, matching the borders and keeping the double-stick tape in place. Pin through the fold line. Stitch on the fold line, beginning at the marked dot and ending at the edge of the border. Remove the tape. Check to make sure your corner lies flat. Trim the seam allowance to 1/4". Press the seam allowance open.

9. Repeat steps 6–8 for the remaining corners.

FINISHING THE QUILT

Refer to "Finishing Techniques" on page 21 for detailed instructions.

1. Layer the quilt top with batting and backing; baste.
2. Quilt as desired. Diana did a fabulous job of outlining the appliqué shapes and creating a feathery design within the background blocks. She filled in the remainder of the blocks with a medium-sized stipple stitch. She added a feather design to the borders to finish off the overall design and tie all the elements together.
3. Bind the quilt edges with the 2 1/4"-wide binding strips.

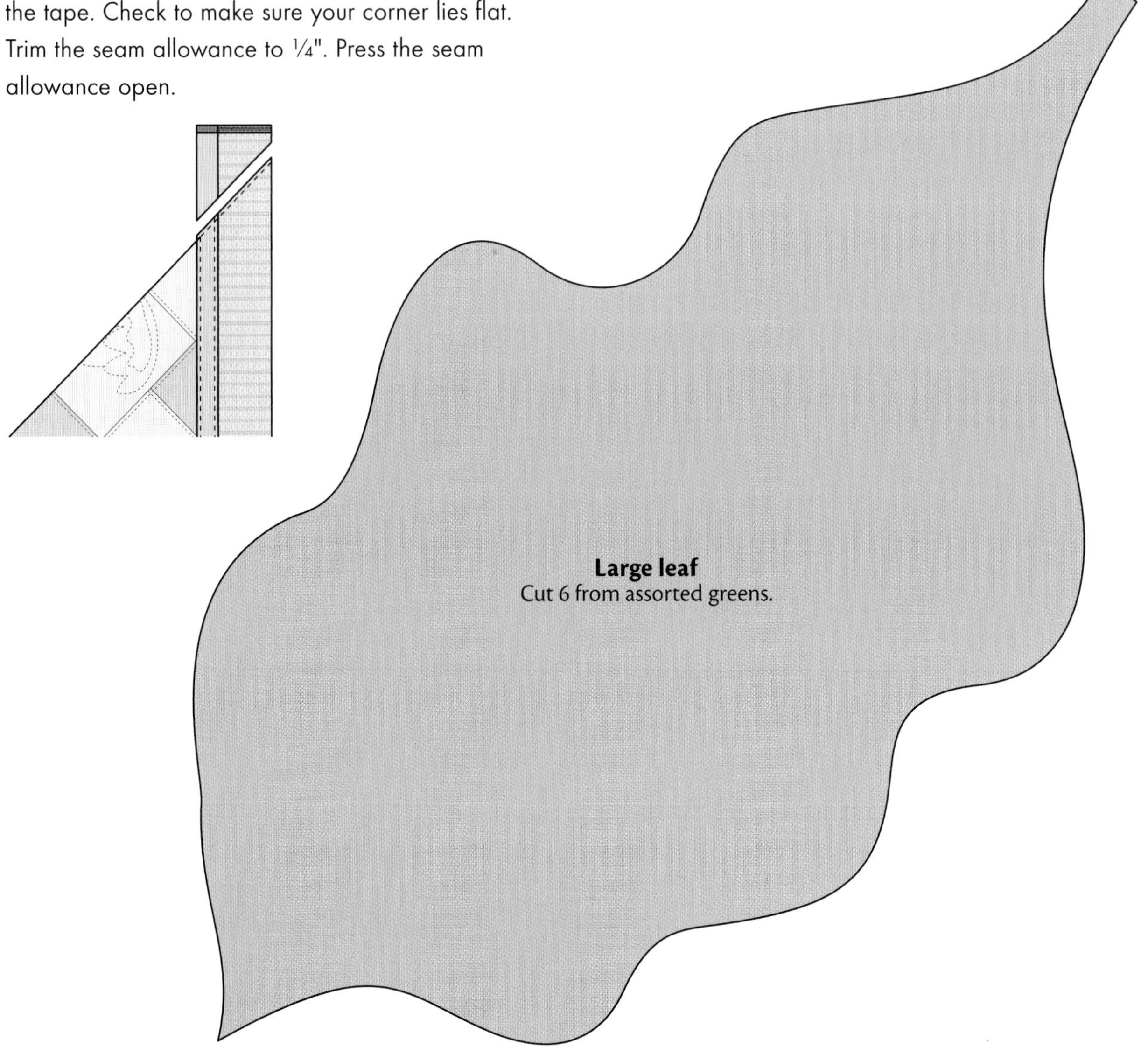

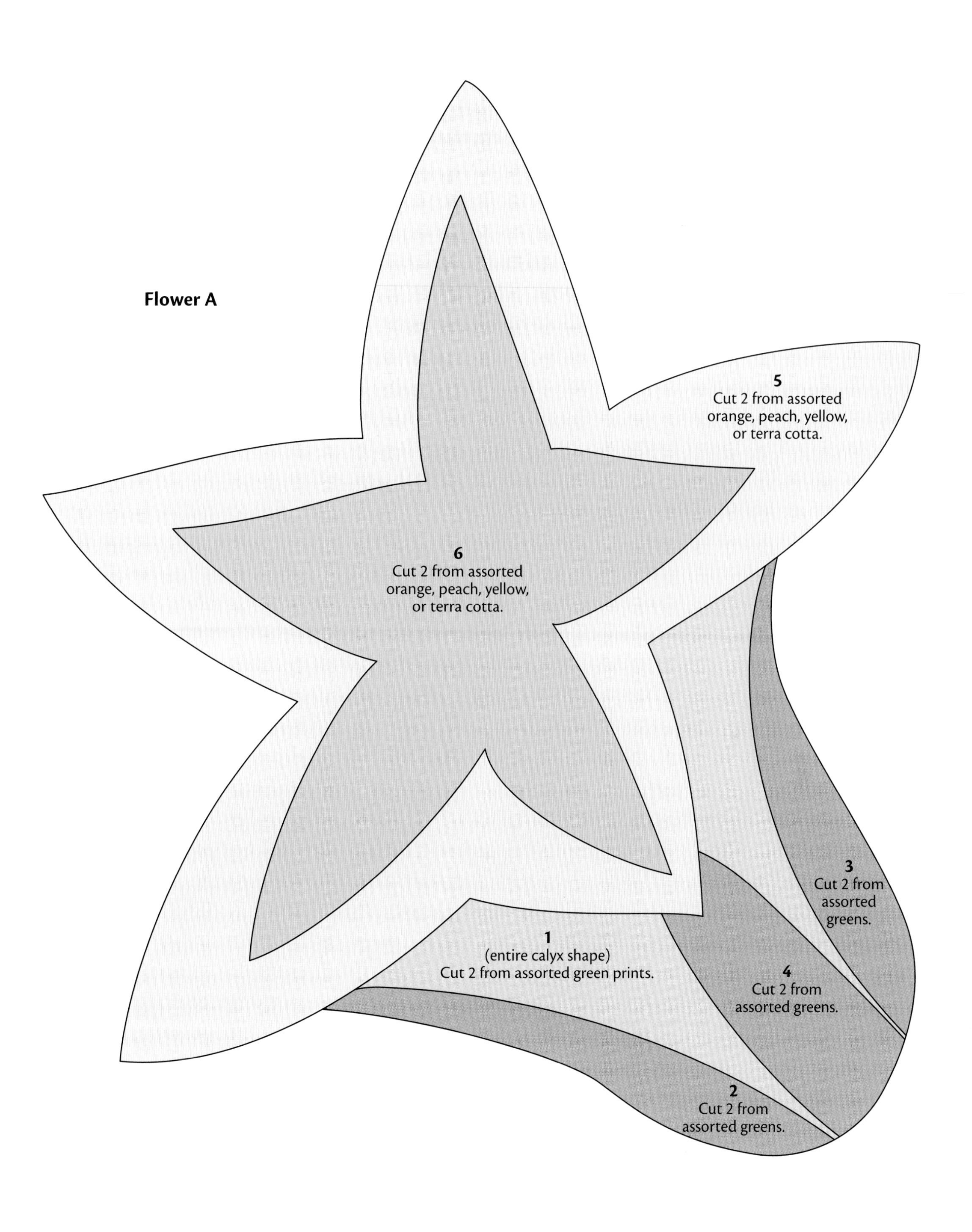
Flower A
5
Cut 2 from assorted
orange, peach, yellow,
or terra cotta.
6
Cut 2 from assorted
orange, peach, yellow,
or terra cotta.
3
Cut 2 from
assorted
greens.
1
(entire calyx shape)
Cut 2 from assorted green prints.
4
Cut 2 from
assorted greens.
2
Cut 2 from
assorted greens.

Flower B

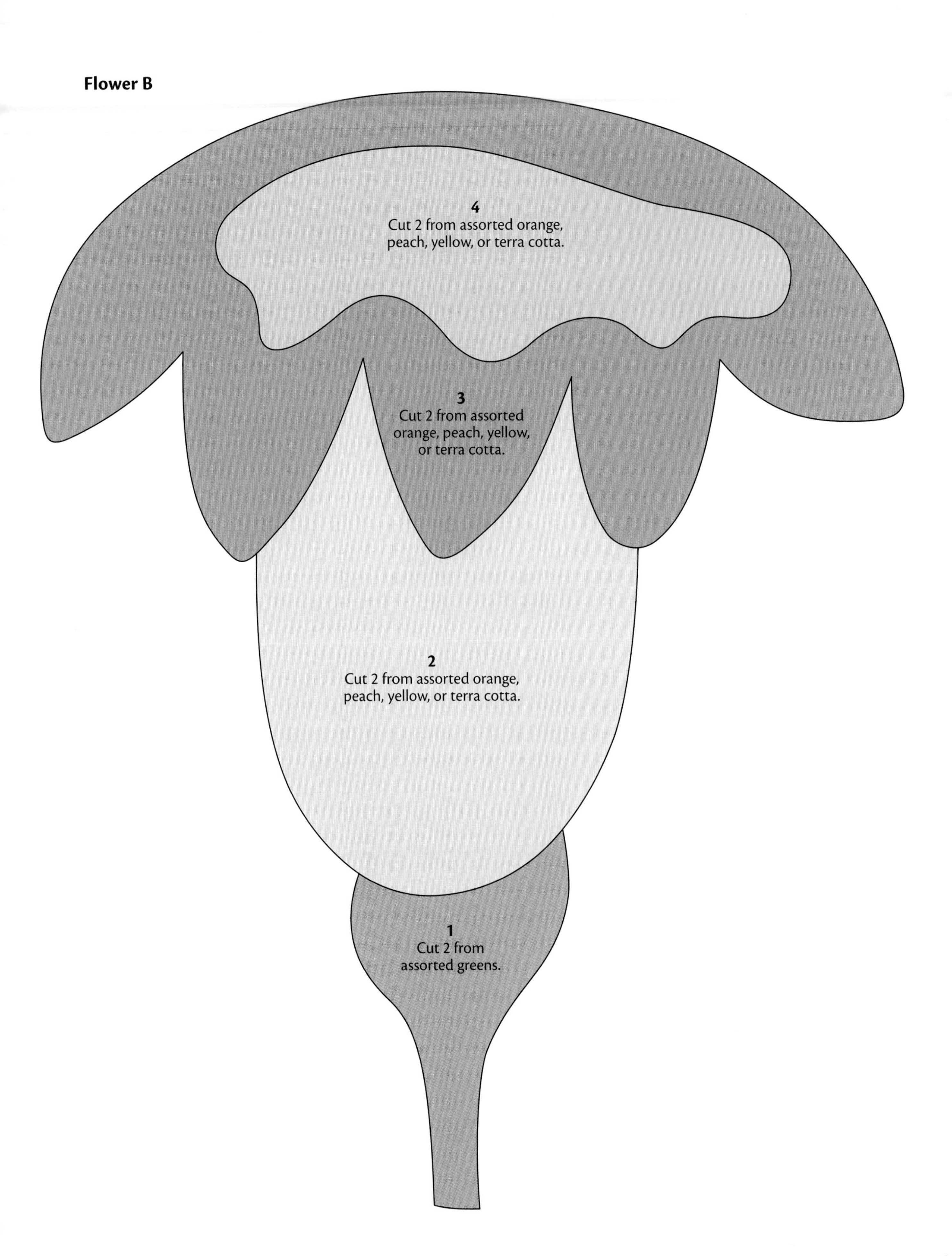
4
Cut 2 from assorted orange, peach, yellow, or terra cotta.
3
Cut 2 from assorted orange, peach, yellow, or terra cotta.
2
Cut 2 from assorted orange, peach, yellow, or terra cotta.
1
Cut 2 from assorted greens.

Pumpkin

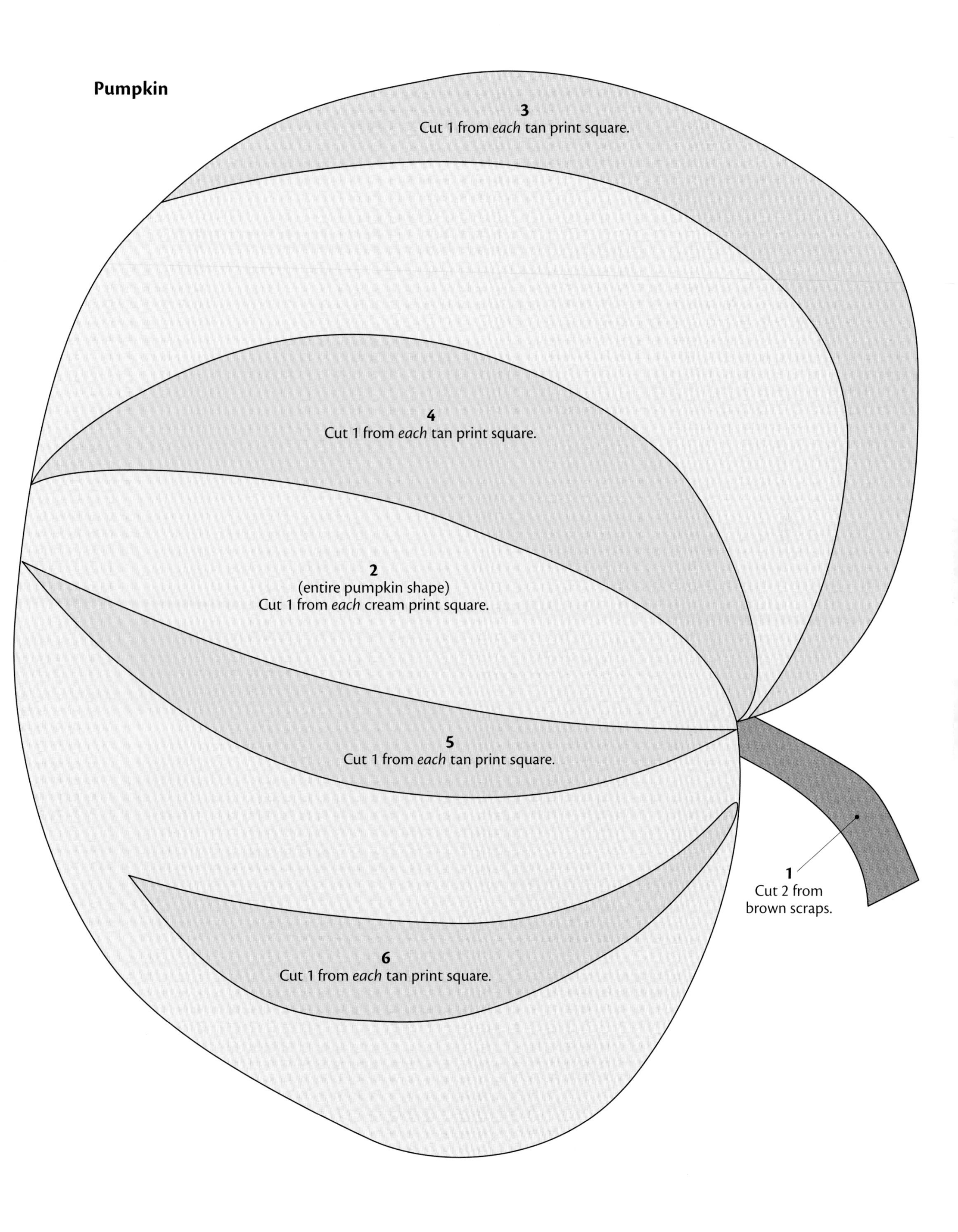

3
Cut 1 from *each* tan print square.
4
Cut 1 from *each* tan print square.
2
(entire pumpkin shape)
Cut 1 from *each* cream print square.
5
Cut 1 from *each* tan print square.
1
Cut 2 from
brown scraps.
6
Cut 1 from *each* tan print square.

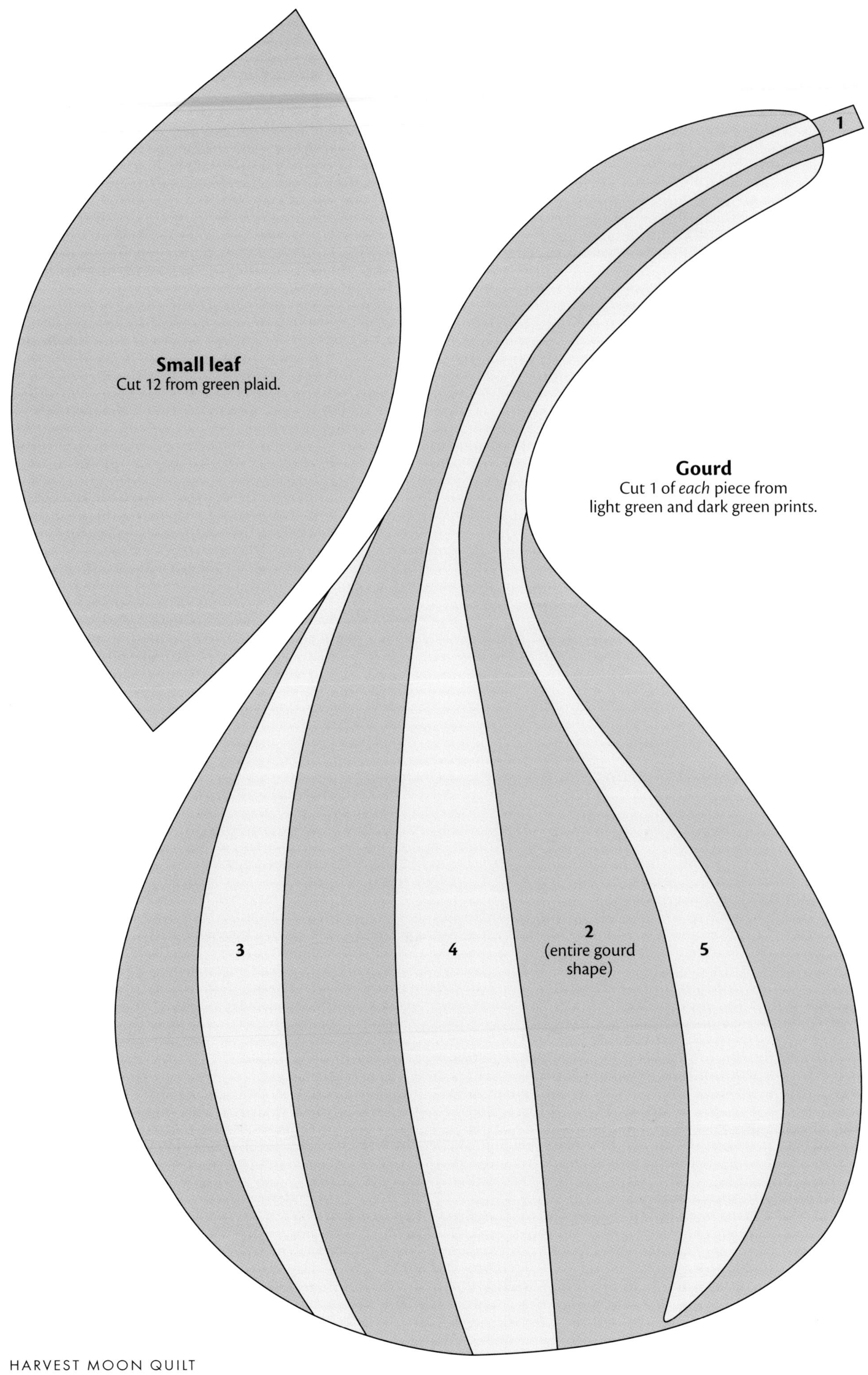
Small leaf
Cut 12 from green plaid.
Gourd
Cut 1 of *each* piece from
light green and dark green prints.
1
3
4
2
(entire gourd
shape)
5

"charming" waist apron

Designed and made by Janis Stob and Margaret Linderman.

This waist-tied apron is made from scraps of all kinds—it's the perfect clean-up-the-sewing-room project! Charm squares are an easy and precoordinated choice, but any grouping of squares from your stash will look wonderful in this easy apron. Reminiscent of your grandma's kitchen, this simple project can be whipped up on a weekend afternoon and ready for cooking on Monday!

—Janis and Margaret

MATERIALS

Yardages are based on 42"-wide fabrics.

1 yard of muslin for lining

½ yard *total* of assorted fabrics for waistband/ties

24 squares of assorted fabrics, 5" x 5", for pieced front

⅛ yard of fabric for front bottom band

1 fat quarter of coordinating print for pocket

1¼ yards of 1"-wide flat lace

1"-diameter button

CUTTING

All measurements include ¼"-wide seam allowances.

From the fabric for the front bottom band, cut:
1 piece, 4½" x 27½"

From the fat quarter for pocket, cut:
2 squares, 8½" x 8½"

From the lace, cut:
1 piece, 27½" long

1 piece, 10" long

From the muslin, cut:
1 piece, 22½" x 27½"

MAKING THE APRON

1. Arrange the 5" squares into four rows of six squares each. Sew the squares in each row together. Press the seam allowances in opposite directions from row to row. Sew the rows together. Press the seam allowances in one direction.

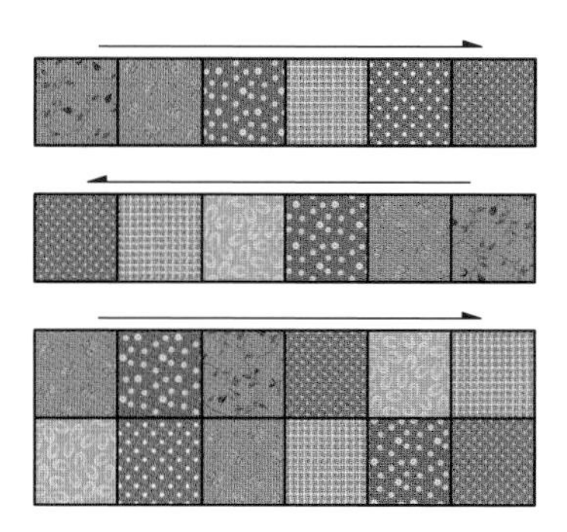

2. With right side up, baste the 27½" piece of lace to one long edge of the bottom band 4½" x 27½" strip. Sew this piece to the step 1 squares, right sides together with the lace edge aligned with the bottom edge of the pieced squares. Press the seam allowance toward the bottom band.

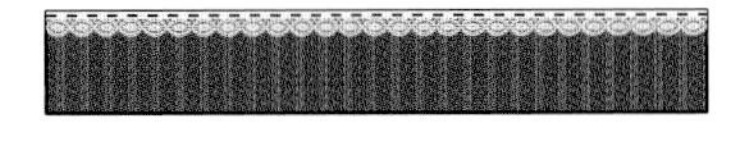

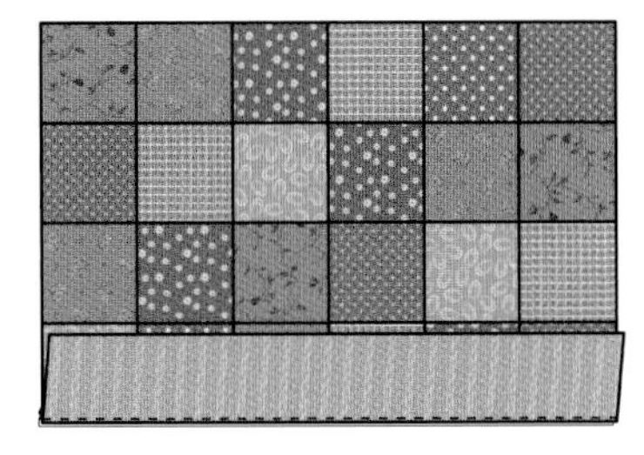

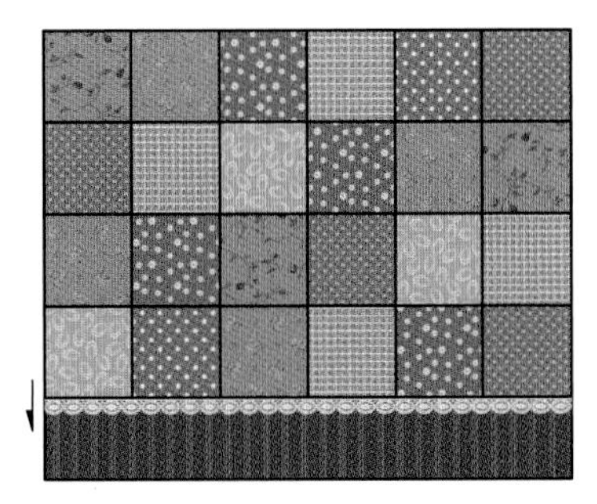

3. To make the pocket, turn under the ends of the 10" lace piece ½" and then ½" again; stitch the turned edges in place. Baste the lace to the corner of one of the 8½" pocket squares as shown, pleating as needed to turn the corner.

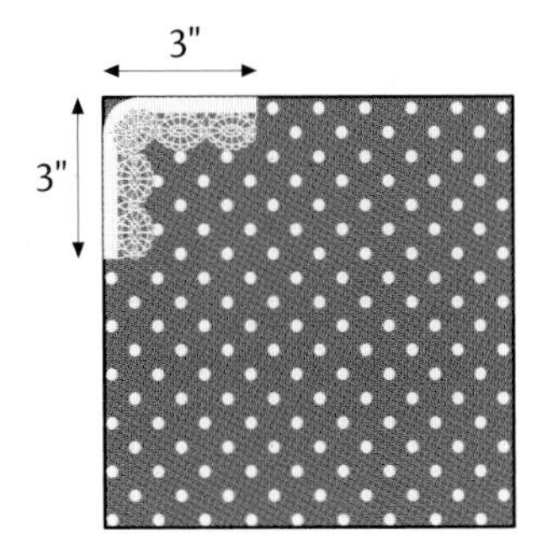

4. Place the remaining pocket square over the lace-trimmed square, right sides together and raw edges aligned. Stitch the squares together, leaving an opening on one of the edges without lace for turning. Turn the pocket right side out and press. Whipstitch the opening closed. Turn down the lace-edged corner and press it in place. Sew the button to the point of the turned back corner, stitching through all the layers.

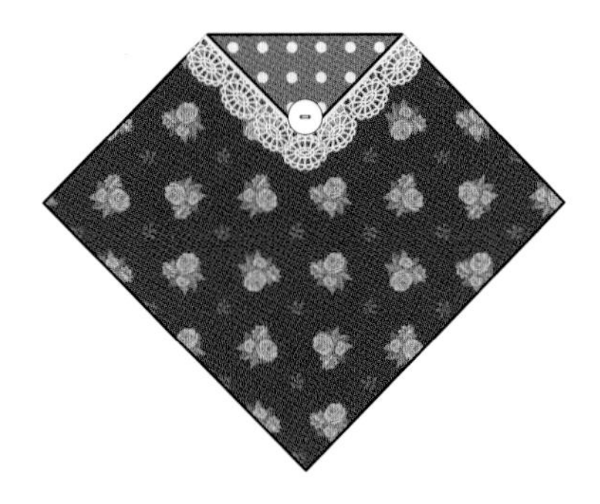

5. Stitch the front and muslin pieces right sides together along the two sides and bottom edge, leaving the top edge open. Turn the apron right side out.
6. Position the pocket on the right-hand side of the apron front on point, with the straight edge of the turned-back corner about 4½" from the top edge and the side point about 3½" from the apron side. Sew the pocket in place along the edges, leaving the turned-back edge free.

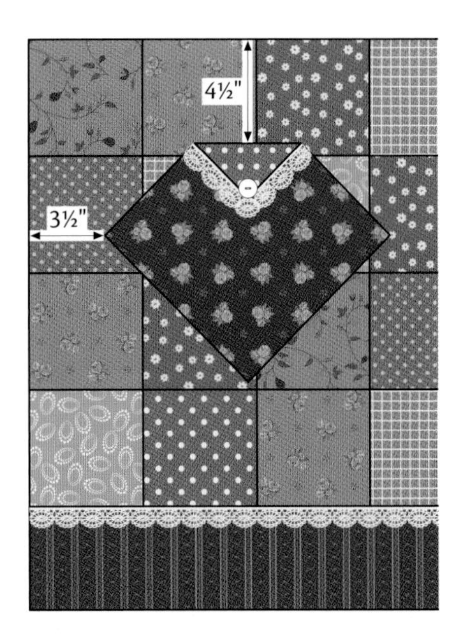

7. Sew two rows of gathering stitches along the top edge of the apron. Evenly gather the top edge to measure 22".

8. To make the waistband, cut the assorted fabrics for the waistband/ties into 2¼"-wide strips of random lengths. Piece them together end to end to make a 124½"-long strip. Press the seam allowances open.

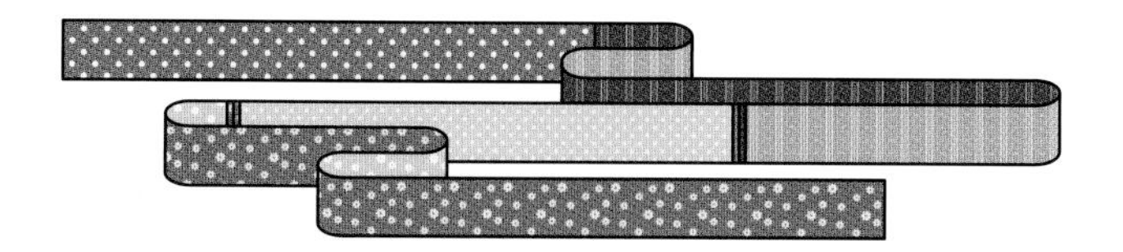

9. With right sides together, sew the ends together to create a circle. Press the seam allowance open. Fold the joined strip in half crosswise at any point; finger-press one of the folds. This will be the center of the strip. Do not turn the piece to the right side.

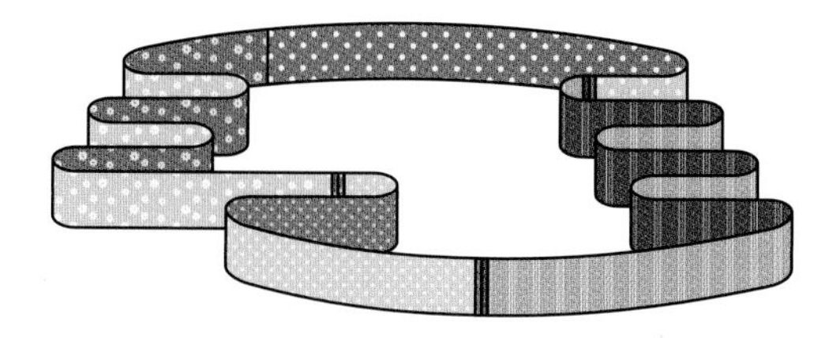

10. Fold the apron in half lengthwise and pin mark the edge at the fold to mark the center point. With right sides together, place the top edge of the apron inside the waistband piece, aligning the top edges and matching center points; pin the pieces together the entire length of the waist. Align the top and bottom edges of the waistband/tie piece that extend beyond both sides of the apron waist and pin them together. Beginning at the side of the apron, stitch away from the waistband along the bottom edge on the tie portion of the piece. Continue stitching up the end, across the top of the waistband/tie piece, and back to the opposite side. Leave the bottom edge of the piece that extends across the apron unstitched.

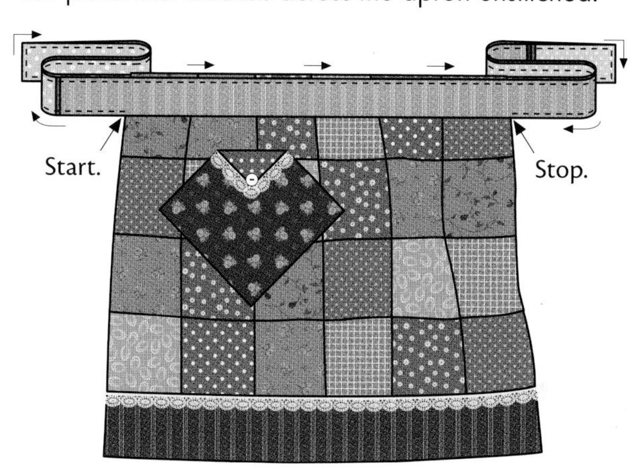

11. Turn the waistband/ties to the right side through the waist opening. Fold the unstitched half of the waistband to the wrong side of the apron. Press the waistband/tie piece, turning under and pressing the seam allowance along the unstitched area of the waist. Whipstitch the waistband in place through the lining only. Topstitch ¼" from the edges around the entire waistband/tie piece.

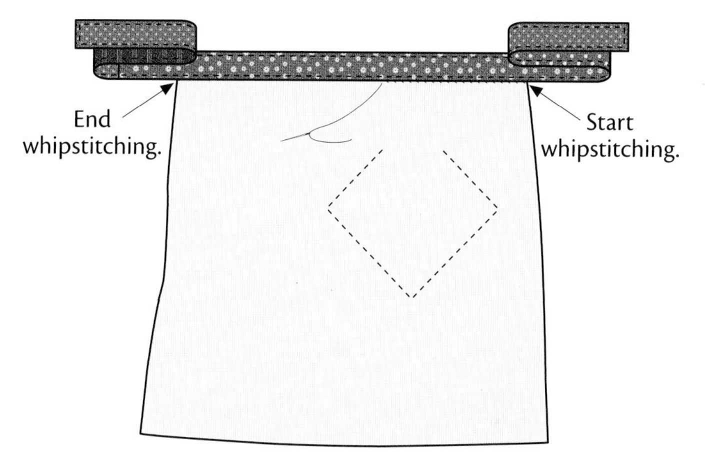

harvest table

Designed and sewn by Jackie Cate.

The inspiration for these seasonal fruit and vegetable pincushions came from visiting our local farmers' market. Fall and winter bring persimmons, pumpkins, gourds, and turnips. The abundance of the harvest—the colors, textures, and tastes of fall—are perfect for the autumn table!

—Jackie

MATERIALS

Amounts given are enough to make one of each vegetable. In addition to the materials given below, you will need the general pincushion supplies listed on page 24.

Persimmon

1 fat eighth of orange or pumpkin-colored fabric

4" x 4" square of green felted wool for calyx

Green thread or floss

½"-diameter brown flat button

Size 11 orange seed beads (optional)

Size 11 straw needle for beading (optional)

Gourd

1 fat eighth *total* of two coordinating fabrics

Twig for stem

Size 11 seed beads to match fabrics (optional)

Size 11 straw needle for beading (optional)

Ribbon or raffia to tie around stem (optional)

Tacky glue

Turnip

1 fat eighth of white, off-white, or cream fabric

2 pieces, 6" x 9", of green cotton fabric for leaves

6" x 9" piece of lightweight paper-backed fusible web

18" of green florist wire

18" of ribbon to tie around leaves

Tacky glue

Large or Small Pumpkin

1 fat quarter *total* of two coordinating orange or pumpkin fabrics OR 1 fat quarter of one fabric

4" x 4" square of green felted wool for leaf OR 1 vintage millinery leaf

Twig or 3" x 3" square of green felted wool for stem

Embroidery floss or size 5 pearl cotton in a color to match pumpkin fabric

Long doll-making needle

Size 11 seed beads to match fabric (optional)

Size 11 straw needle for beading (optional)

Ribbon to tie around stem (optional)

Tacky glue

ASSEMBLING THE PINCUSHIONS

Refer to "Basic Pincushion Instructions" on page 24.

Persimmon

1. Use the patterns on page 58 to make freezer-paper templates for the persimmon and calyx. Cut out the persimmon pieces from the orange or pumpkin-colored fabric and the calyxes from the green wool square. Mark the starting and stopping points on the wrong side of each persimmon piece.
2. With right sides together, stitch the persimmon pieces together side by side, starting and stopping where indicated. Stitch the end pieces together to form the shape, stitching from mark to mark as before. Make sure your points at the bottom match and that the bottom is closed. There will be an opening at the top. Turn the piece right side out and stuff it.

3. Use the hand-quilting thread to make a running stitch around the opening at the top, leaving a 4" tail on both ends. Pull the thread ends to gather the opening (it will not be completely closed), and then tie the ends together and knot twice.
4. Place the four calyx shapes at the top of the persimmon so they slightly overlap each other and cover the opening. Use matching thread or one strand of floss to whipstitch the calyxes in place.
5. Center the button over the calyxes and sew it in place. Add beads to the seams, if desired.

Gourd

1. Use the pattern on page 58 to make freezer-paper templates. Cut three shapes from one of the fabrics and three reversed shapes from the other fabric. Mark the starting and stopping points on the wrong side of each piece.
2. With right sides together, sew one shape from each fabric together along the straight edge from the top to the bottom. Repeat to make a total of three pairs.

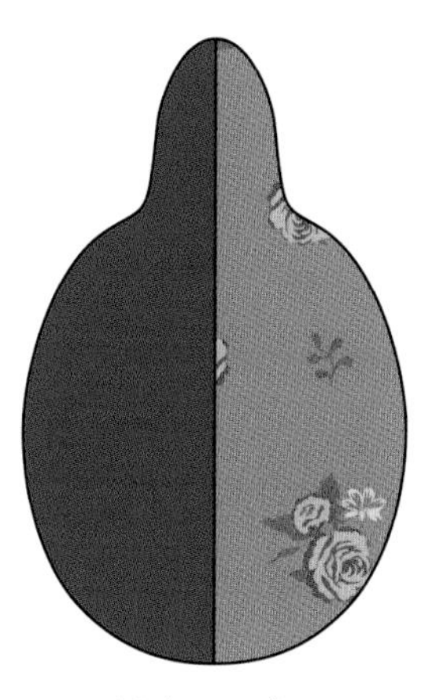

Make 3 pairs.

3. Sew the pairs together side by side, starting and stopping where indicated. Bring the left- and right-hand pieces right sides together and stitch from mark to mark as before. There will be an opening at the top. Turn the piece right side out and stuff it.

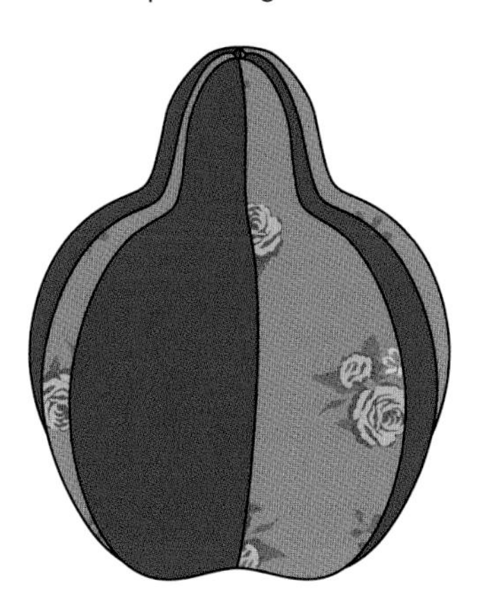

4. Use the hand-quilting thread to make a running stitch around the opening at the top, leaving a 4" tail on both ends. Insert the twig into the opening, apply some glue around it, and then pull the threads to gather the fabric around the twig. Knot the thread ends twice and cut off the excess thread.
5. If desired, add beads to the seams and tie a length of ribbon or raffia around the stem.

Turnip

1. Use the patterns on page 58 to make freezer-paper templates for the turnip and turnip leaves. Cut out the turnip pieces from the white, off-white, or cream fabric. Do not cut out the leaves yet.
2. Sew the turnip pieces together side by side. Bring the end pieces together and sew to form the shape, leaving an opening at the top. Turn the piece right side out and stuff it, placing a small bit of cotton stuffing into the point first so it keeps its shape.

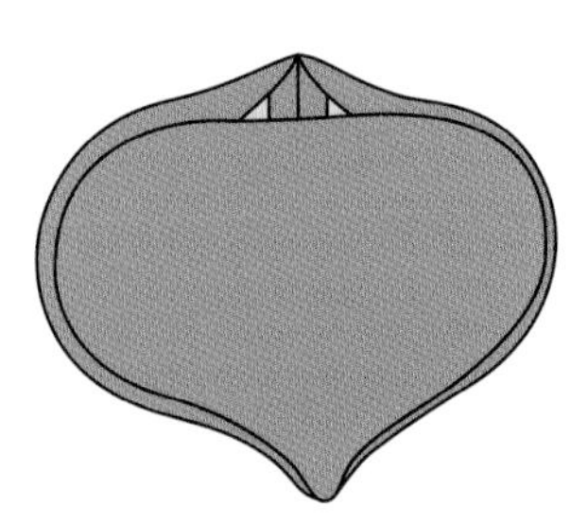

3. Use the hand-quilting thread to make a running stitch around the opening at the top, leaving a 4" tail on both ends. Pull the thread ends to gather the opening so that it is almost closed. You will need to leave a small opening to insert the end of each leaf into the opening. Tie the thread ends together and knot twice. Cut off the excess thread.
4. To make the leaves, iron the fusible web piece to the wrong side of one of the green pieces. Remove the paper. Iron the freezer-paper leaf templates to the wrong side of the remaining green piece, leaving approximately ½" between each shape; trace around them and then remove the templates.
5. Pin the green pieces right sides together. Sew on the traced lines. Cut out the leaf shapes ¼" from the stitching lines. Clip the inner curves, and then turn each leaf right side out. *Do not press them.*
6. Cut the florist wire into three 6" lengths. Place a wire into each leaf, centering it as much as possible. Carefully press the leaf, fusing the two sides together with the wire between the layers. Trim the excess wire.
7. Put a small amount of glue into the opening of the turnip. Insert the open end of the leaves into the opening, working them down into the turnip so they are relatively stable. To further secure the leaves, stitch them in place. Thread a needle with hand-quilting thread, bury the knot in the seam on one side of the opening, and then stitch through the bottom of the leaf ends that are inside the turnip, coming out at the other seam. Insert the needle back through the seam near where you came out, through the leaf ends, and back out through the other seam. Repeat this process several times until the leaves are secure.
8. Shape the leaves as desired, and tie the ribbon in a bow around the leaves at the top of the turnip.

Quick-and-Easy Leaves

Instead of the wired fabric leaves, you can make leaves from ribbon.

1. Cut four 9" lengths of ½"-wide ribbon.
2. Lay the ribbons on top of each other and fold them in half crosswise to find the center. Place the center point over the opening of the turnip in a pleasing manner. You can leave them on top of each other or fan them out.
3. Hand stitch through the center of the ribbons to attach them to the top of the turnip. Sew a button to the top of the turnip over the ribbons.

Pumpkin

The instructions are the same for the small or large pumpkin.

1. Use the patterns on page 59 to make freezer-paper templates for the desired-size pumpkin and the corresponding leaf. Cut out half of the pumpkin shapes from one fabric and the other half from the coordinating fabric, or cut all the pieces from one fabric. If you are making a wool leaf, cut the leaf shapes from the green wool 4" square.
2. Sew the pumpkin pieces side by side, right sides together, alternating the fabrics if you are using two fabrics. Stitch from the point at the bottom to the top, leaving the straight end open. Stitch the end pieces together to form the shape. There will be an opening at the top; make sure the seams at the bottom are completely closed. Turn the piece right side out and stuff it.

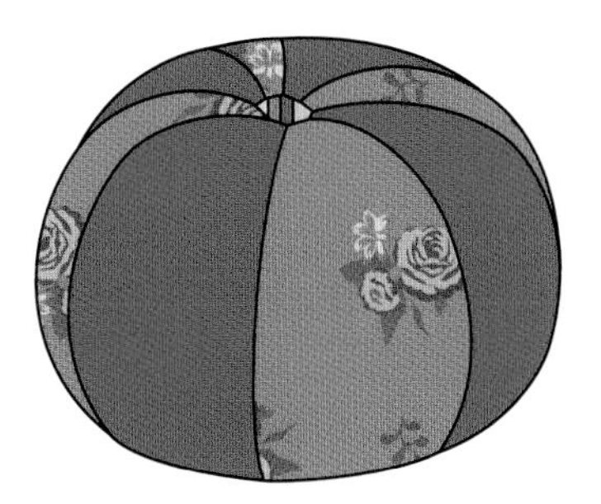

3. Use the hand-quilting thread to make a running stitch around the opening at the top, leaving a 4" tail on both ends. Partially close the opening, leaving some room for a stem. Insert some cotton batting in the opening so the hulls don't fall out.
4. Thread the doll-making needle with pearl cotton or six strands of floss. Knot the thread at one end. Insert the needle at the top of the pumpkin and bring it out the bottom, pulling the thread to bury the knot. Insert the needle back into the top and out the bottom, wrapping the thread or floss along one of the seam lines. Continue to do this until all the seam lines have been covered. Knot the thread and bury it inside the pumpkin.
5. If you are using a twig for the stem, apply some glue to the end of it and insert it into the opening. If you prefer a wool stem, refer to "Stems" on page 25 to make the stem from the green 3" wool square, apply some glue to the end of it, and insert it into the opening. Once your stem is in place, pull the threads to gather the fabric around it. Knot the thread ends twice and cut off the excess thread.
6. If desired, add beads to the seams, placing them over the thread detail.
7. Refer to "Leaves" on page 26 to make the wool leaf. Stem stitch (see page 28) a vein through the center of the leaf. Apply the leaf to the top of the pumpkin near the stem. If you are using a millinery leaf, wrap the wire around the stem to secure it and then tie a length of ribbon around the stem to hide the wire.

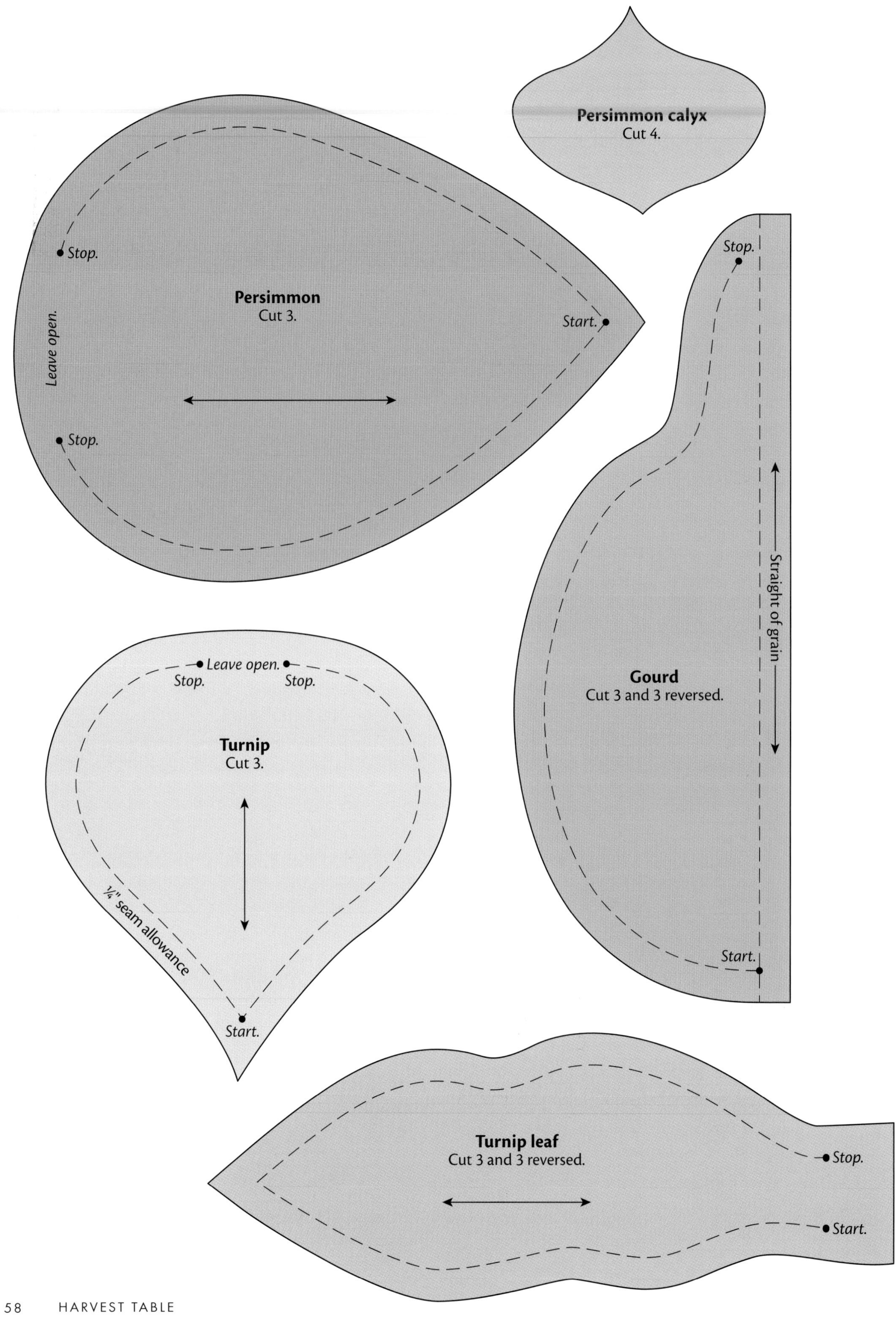
Persimmon calyx
Cut 4.
Stop.
Persimmon
Cut 3.
Start.
Leave open.
Stop.
Stop.
Straight of grain
Leave open.
Stop.
Stop.
Gourd
Cut 3 and 3 reversed.
Turnip
Cut 3.
¼" seam allowance
Start.
Start.
Turnip leaf
Cut 3 and 3 reversed.
Stop.
Start.

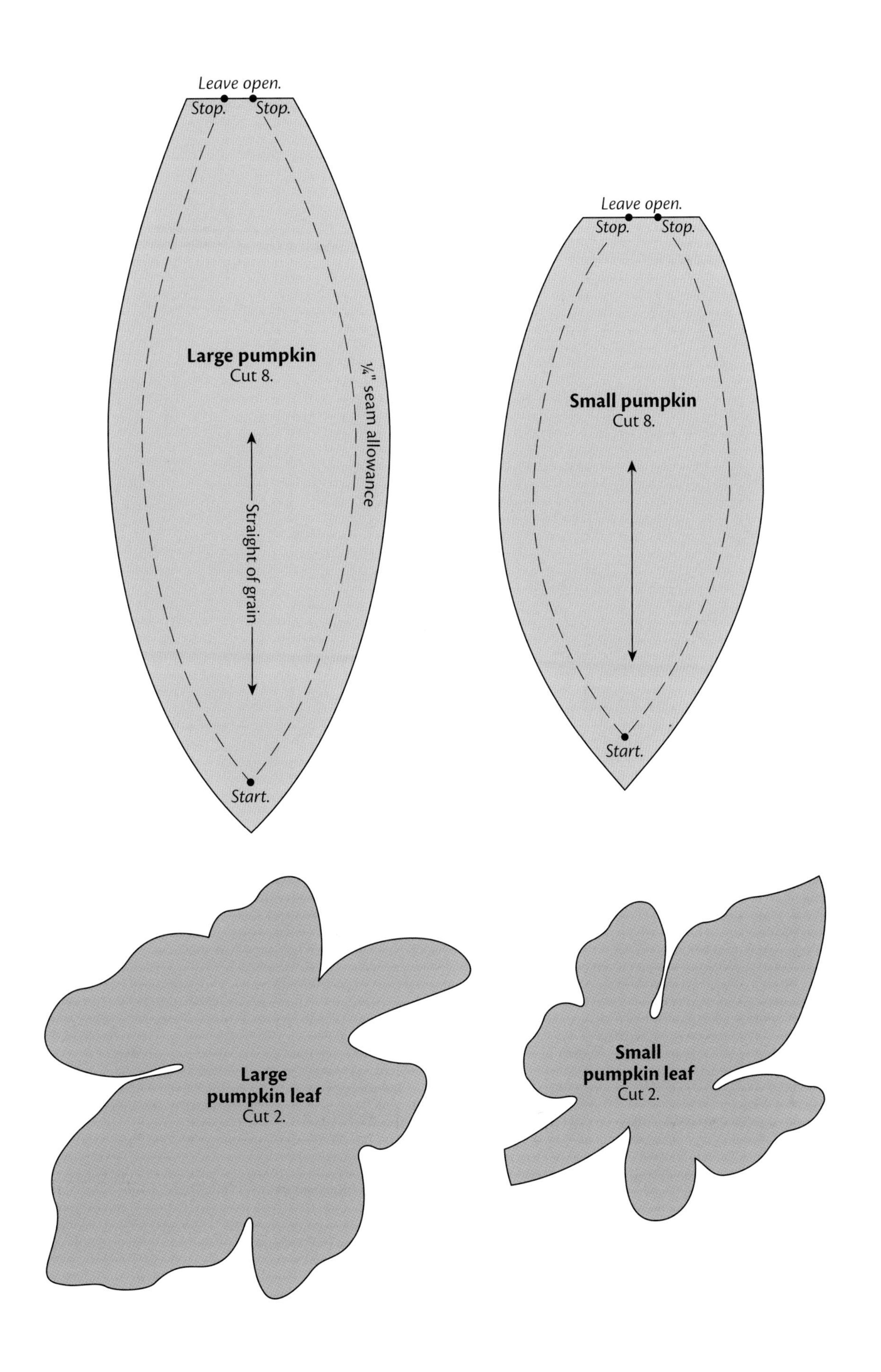
Leave open.
Stop.
Stop.
Large pumpkin
Cut 8.
¼" seam allowance
Straight of grain
Start.
Leave open.
Stop.
Stop.
Small pumpkin
Cut 8.
Start.
Large
pumpkin leaf
Cut 2.
Small
pumpkin leaf
Cut 2.

Kitchen Comforts

This colorful collection is meant to take you way back . . . to those fun-loving 1950s with the red-checkered tiles, the spinning bar stools, and the colorful kitchen appliances. Just tying a whimsical apron around your waist, like the one shown on page 74, will transport you to the sensation of being a bona fide '50's housewife cooking up some afternoon goodies for her family! Add in a few specially made "veggies," a summery tablecloth, and an easy-to-make recipe book, and who knows where this collection might lead you.

a 1950's summer tablecloth

Doesn't this tablecloth just make you want to run out and get a picnic basket and fill it up with wonderful little morsels of cheese, bread, olives, and sausage, and top it off with a bottle of good wine? No opportunity to picnic outside? That's okay, this is a perfect chance to have an indoor picnic. Our family regularly gathers on the living room floor and puts out our own version of an indoor picnic. The kids absolutely love it, and it gives us a great chance to reconnect as a family and do something different and fun. Can you think of a good time to have your own living-room picnic?

—Joanna

Finished quilt size: 60" diameter

MATERIALS

Yardages are based on 42"-wide fabrics.

½ yard *each* of 2 assorted red prints (1 and 2), 3 assorted green prints (1–3), and 4 assorted cream prints (1–4)

⅜ yard of cream print 6

⅓ yard of cream print 5

⅓ yard of red print 3

¾ yard of green print 4 for binding

3¾ yards of fabric for backing

CUTTING

All measurements include ¼"-wide seam allowances.

From *each* of red prints 1 and 2, cut:

1 strip, 5½" x 42" (2 total); crosscut *each* strip into 4 squares, 5½" x 5½" (8 total)

From *each* of red prints 1–3, cut:

1 strip, 8" x 42" (3 total); crosscut *each* strip into 5 squares, 8" x 8" (15 total; you'll have 3 extra)

From *each* of green prints 1–3, cut:

1 strip, 5½" x 42" (3 total); crosscut 2 strips *each* into 2 squares, 5½" x 5½"; crosscut the remaining strip into 4 squares, 5½" x 5½" (8 total)

1 strip, 8" x 42" (3 total); crosscut *each* strip into 4 squares, 8" x 8" (12 total; you'll have 2 extra)

From *each* of cream prints 1–4, cut:

1 strip, 5½" x 42" (4 total); crosscut each strip into 3 squares, 5½" x 5½" (12 total)

From *each* of cream prints 1–5, cut:

1 strip, 8" x 42" (5 total); crosscut *each* strip into 5 squares, 8" x 8" (25 total; you'll have 3 extra)

From cream print 6, cut:

2 strips, 5½" x 42"; crosscut *each* strip into 2 pieces, 5½" x 20½" (4 total)

Designed and sewn by Joanna Figueroa; quilted by Diana Johnson.

PIECING THE TABLECLOTH TOP

1. Press four cream 5½" square in half diagonally, wrong sides together. Lay one square on top of a red 5½" square. Sew on the fold line. Cut the excess off the back, ¼" from the stitching line. Press the seam allowance toward the red triangle. Repeat to make a total of four triangle-square units using two different red prints and three or four different cream prints. Repeat to make four green-and-cream triangle-square units using three different green prints and a variety of cream prints.

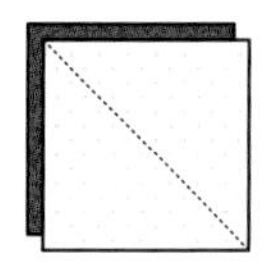
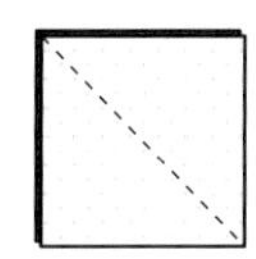
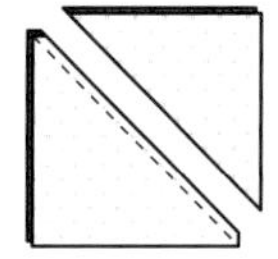

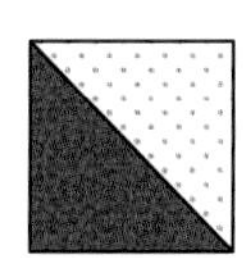
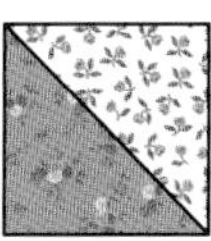

Make 4 of each.

2. Arrange the red triangle-square units into two rows of two squares each. Make sure the same red triangles oppose each other. Sew the squares in each row together. Press the seam allowances in opposite directions. Sew the rows together. Press the seam allowance in either direction.

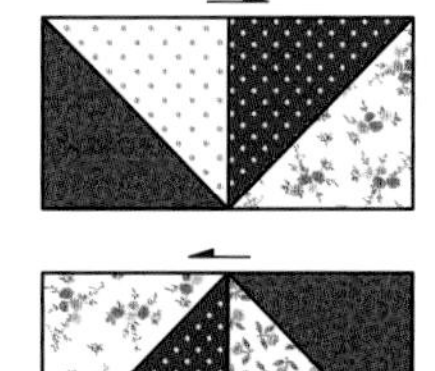

3. Lay out the four green triangle-squares from step 1, four green 5½" squares that match the triangle-square units, and four assorted cream 5½" squares as shown so that each green square is next to the matching triangle square. Sew the pieces together in three vertical rows. Press the seam allowances as indicated. Sew the rows together. Press the seam allowances in either direction.

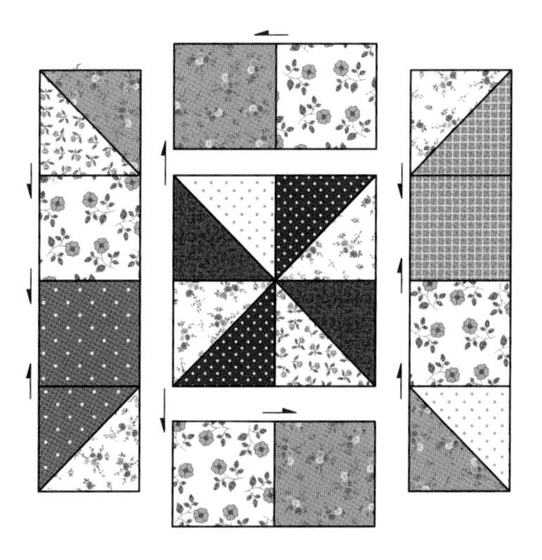

4. Sew a cream 5½" x 20½" piece to each side of the pinwheel unit from step 3. Press the seam allowances away from the pinwheel unit. Add a red 5½" square to the ends of the two remaining 5½" x 20½" strips. Press the seam allowances toward the cream pieces. Add these strips to the top and bottom of the pinwheel unit. Press the seam allowances away from the pinwheel unit.

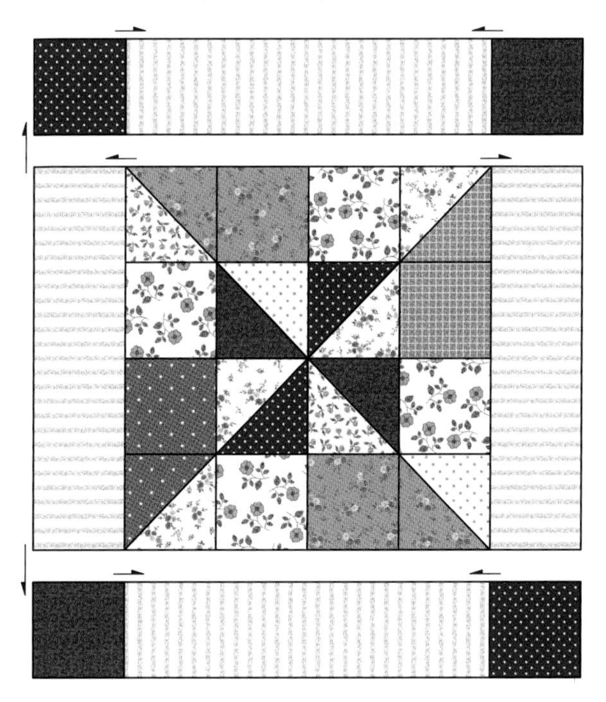

5. Randomly select two cream and two green 8" squares and sew them together, alternating colors. Repeat to make a second strip. Refer to the quilt assembly diagram to sew the strips to the top and bottom of the quilt top, paying careful attention to color placement. Press the seam allowances away from the quilt top.
6. Repeat step 5 to make two strips, each with three green and three cream squares. Sew these strips to the sides of the quilt top as shown. Press the seam allowances away from the quilt top.
7. Repeat step 5 to make four strips, each with three red and three cream squares. Refer to the assembly diagram to sew two of the strips to the top and bottom of the quilt top. Press the seam allowances away from the quilt top. Sew the remaining two strips to the sides of the quilt top as shown. Press the seam allowances away from the quilt top.

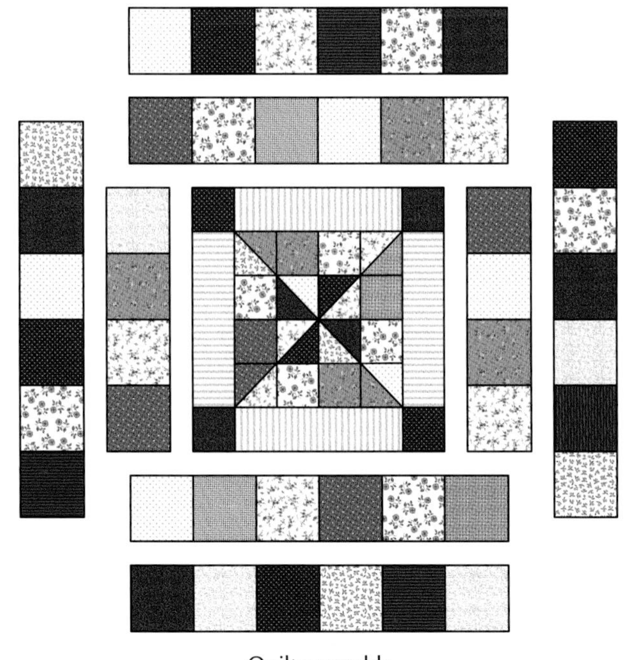

Quilt assembly

FINISHING THE TABLECLOTH

Refer to "Finishing Techniques" on page 21 for detailed instructions.

1. Layer the quilt top and backing; baste. Because this is a tablecloth, and you want it to drape easily over the table, there is no batting. If desired, you could use a very thin batting, such as Thermore, or a piece of flannel to add a little body. If you'll be using your tablecloth on the ground for outdoor picnics or as a blanket, by all means add batting and create a normal quilt sandwich.
2. Quilt as desired. If you aren't using any batting, you will most likely need to experiment with your tension to get your thread to accommodate the lack of batting in your project. Diana chose a wonderful feathery allover design—one of her signature designs actually—and used a cream-colored thread, which always seems to give my quilts the vintage look I want.

3. Cut a piece of string approximately 35" long and tie one end to a small lead pencil or chalk pencil. Measure 30½" from the pencil and place a pin in the string at that point. Place the pin in the center of the pinwheel unit and stretch the string taut. It should hit the edge of your quilt at the center of the top, bottom, and sides. Using the string as your compass and keeping it stretched taut, trace a circle all the way around the quilt.
4. Cut out the circle on the marked line.
5. Refer to "Cutting Bias Strips" on page 27 to cut the green print 4 fabric into 2¼"-wide strips. You will need enough strips to equal 250" when pieced together. Stitch the strips together and bind the tablecloth edges, taking care to not pull on your binding when attaching it so that your edges don't curl after binding.

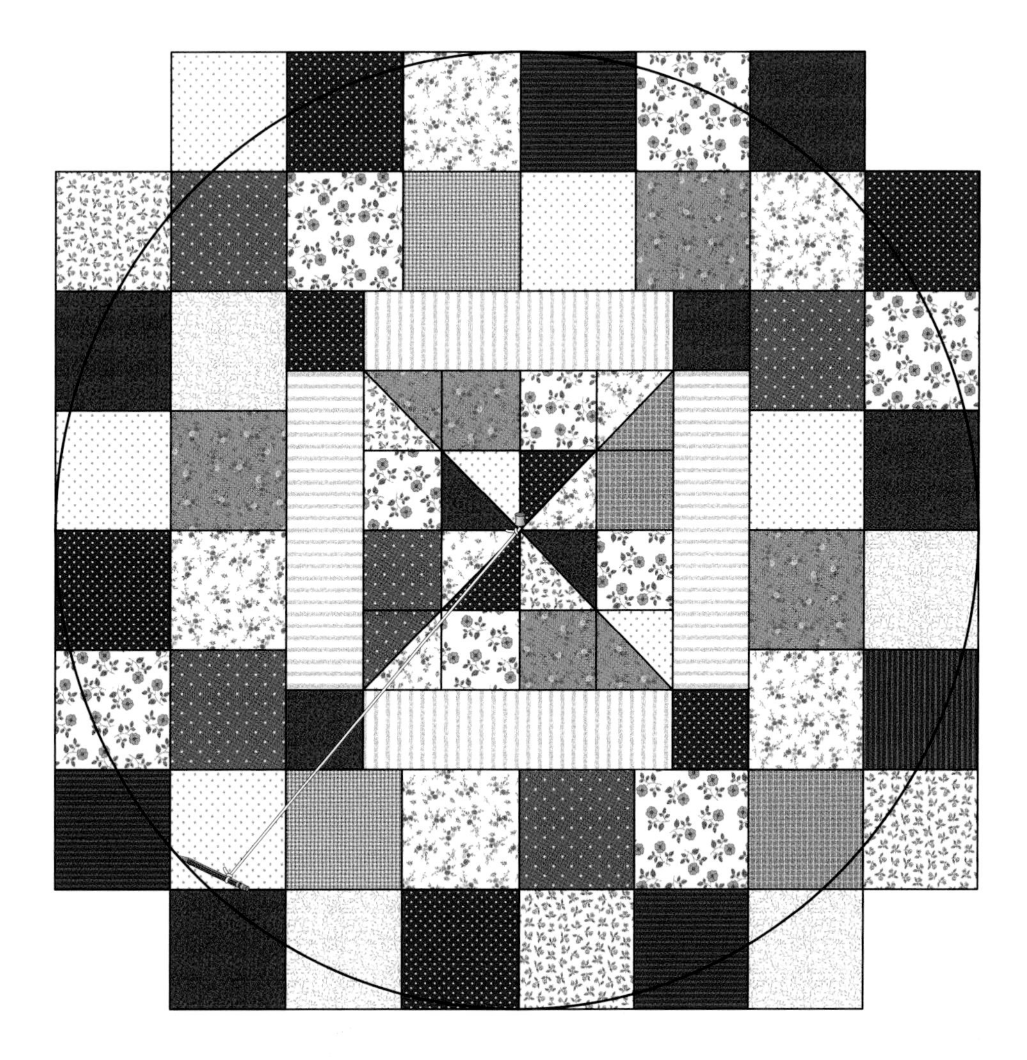

kitchen garden

Designed and sewn by Jackie Cate.

When I was a little girl, my grandmother Eliza had a beautiful kitchen garden in our backyard. I loved helping her and picking all of the wonderful fresh vegetables to cook with. I enjoyed all the bright, wonderful colors in the vegetables. I hope to have a kitchen garden myself one day. For now, I enjoy going to the farmers' market and choosing the beautiful produce to create vignettes on my table or counter top. I designed these pincushions so I could enjoy summer vegetables all year long.

—Jackie

MATERIALS

Amounts given are enough to make one of each vegetable. In addition to the materials given below, you will need the general pincushion supplies listed on page 24.

Tomato

1 fat quarter *total* of two coordinating fabrics OR 1 fat quarter of 1 fabric (you can use whatever color you desire)

4" x 4" scrap of green felted wool for calyx

Scrap of cream felted wool for flower (optional)

Scrap of yellow felted wool for flower center (optional)

Green embroidery floss or size 5 pearl cotton

Long doll-making needle

Carrot

8" x 8" square of orange wool

12" of 2½"-wide green wired ribbon OR 4" x 12" piece of green felted wool for leaves

Chalk pencil (optional)

Size 11 orange seed beads (optional)

Size 11 straw needle (optional)

Patty Pan Squash

2 squares, 4" x 4", of white, yellow, or green fabrics (you can use a different fabric for each square.)

Coordinating embroidery floss for topstitching detail

Small button

Eggplant

1 fat quarter *total* of two coordinating purple fabrics OR 1 fat quarter of 1 fabric

5" x 5" square of green felted wool for calyx and stem

Green thread or embroidery floss

Size 11 purple seed beads (optional)

Size 11 straw needle (optional)

Tacky glue

ASSEMBLING THE PINCUSHIONS

Refer to "Basic Pincushion Instructions" on page 24.

Tomato

The instructions are the same for the small or large tomato.

1. Use the patterns on page 70 to make freezer-paper templates for the desired-size tomato and the tomato calyx. Cut out half of the tomato shapes from one fabric and the other half from the coordinating fabric, or cut all the pieces from one fabric. Cut the calyx from the green wool square.

   If you are making the optional tomato flower, make templates for the flower and flower center. Cut the flower piece from the white scrap and the flower center from the yellow scrap.

2. Sew the tomato pieces side by side, right sides together, alternating the fabrics if you are using two fabrics. Stitch from the point at the bottom to the top, leaving the straight end open. Stitch the end pieces together to form the shape. There will be an opening at the top; make sure the seams at the bottom are completely closed. Turn the piece right side out and stuff it.

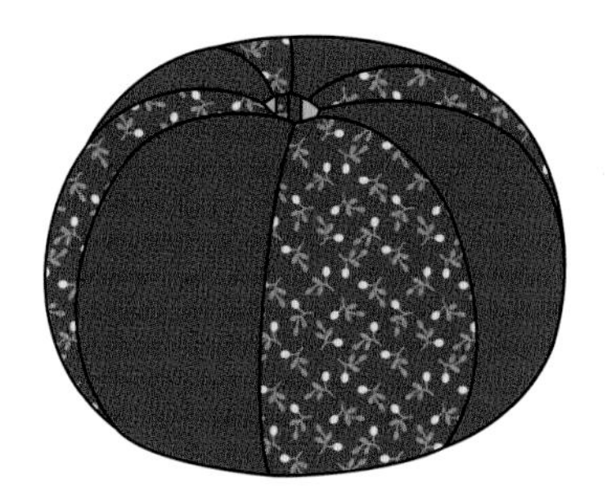

3. Use the hand-quilting thread to make a running stitch around the opening at the top, leaving a 4" tail on both ends. Pull the thread ends to close the opening, and then tie the ends together in a knot twice.

4. Thread the doll-making needle with pearl cotton or six strands of floss. Knot the thread at one end. Insert the needle at the top of the tomato and out the bottom, pulling the thread to bury the knot. Insert the needle back into the top and out the bottom, wrapping the thread along one of the seam lines. Continue to do this until all the seam lines have been covered. Knot the thread and bury it inside the tomato.

> **FRESH TIP**
>
> If you are having difficulty pulling the needle through the pincushion, grab it with your hemostat.

5. Position the calyx over the top of the tomato. At this point, you have two options for finishing the top. If you just want to add the calyx, center it over the top of the tomato. Thread the doll-making needle with pearl cotton or six strands of embroidery floss, and knot the thread at one end. Insert the needle

into the bottom of the tomato and out the center of the calyx, pulling the knot into the pincushion to bury it. Insert the needle back into the pincushion near where it came out, and out the bottom. Come back up through the top and out through the bottom again, leaving a loop of the desired size at the top. Knot the thread and pull the knot into the pincushion to bury it.

If you want to add the flower to the center of the calyx, whipstitch (see page 28) the center to the flower with matching thread. Center the flower on the calyx and repeat the instructions above using pearl cotton or just two strands of embroidery floss and omitting the loop.

Carrot

The instructions are the same for the small or large carrot.

1. Use the pattern on page 71 to make freezer-paper templates for the desired-size carrot. Cut out the pieces from the orange fabric.
2. Sew the carrot pieces right sides together, leaving the top edge open. Sew from the bottom to the top to form a cone shape.
3. Turn the piece right side out. Place a small bit of cotton stuffing into the tip first so it keeps its shape, and then fill almost to the top with crushed walnut hulls. Add more cotton stuffing to the top.
4. Use hand-quilting thread to make a running stitch around the opening at the top, leaving a 6" tail on both ends. Pull the thread ends to close the opening. Knot the thread ends twice and cut off the excess thread.
5. You have two options for finishing the top. If you want to finish with a ribbon bow, pinch the ribbon together at the center. Place the center of the ribbon over the top of the carrot and hand tack it in place, going over the ribbon several times to secure it. Once it's firmly attached, tie the bow into a pleasing shape.

   If you prefer the wool leaves, refer to "Quick-and- Easy Leaves" on page 57, cutting 4 strips measuring 1/4" x 12" from the green wool with a wave-edge blade or pinking blade in your rotary cutter.
6. To add the optional bead details, lightly mark some horizontal lines on the carrot where you want to apply the beads. Stitch the beads in place along each marked line, placing the beads as close together as possible. When you are through stitching one line, if there is enough thread left on your needle, insert your needle into the carrot and come up at the next line and continue beading.

Patty Pan Squash

The instructions are the same for the small or large squash.

1. Use the pattern on page 73 to make a freezer-paper template for the desired-size squash.
2. Iron the template to the wrong side of one of the pieces. Trace around the shape, and then remove the template.
3. Place the fabric square and the marked square right sides together with the marked square on top. Stitch on the marked line, leaving an opening where indicated. Trim 1/4" from the sewn line. Clip the inner curves.

FRESH TIP

If you have an open-toe foot, use it so you can see the drawn line better. Also, engage the needle-down feature so that you can start and stop as you stitch around the shape without the fabric shifting.

4. Turn the piece right side out and stuff it. Whipstitch (see page 28) the opening closed.
5. Refer to the pattern to stem stitch or backstitch the details on the top of the squash. Center the button on the top of the squash and sew it in place.

Eggplant

1. Use the patterns on page 72 to make freezer-paper templates for the eggplant and calyx. Cut out the eggplant pieces from the purple fabrics, cutting one piece from each of the coordinating fabrics or all of the pieces from one fabric. Cut out the calyx and a 1¼" x 2" piece from the green wool square.
2. With right sides together, stitch the eggplant pieces together side by side, starting and stopping where indicated. Stitch the end pieces together to form the shape, stitching from mark to mark as before. Make sure the points at the bottom match and that the bottom is closed. There will be an opening at the top. Turn the piece right side out and stuff it.

3. Use hand-quilting thread to make a running stitch around the opening at the top, leaving a 4" tail at both ends. Pull the thread ends to gather the opening, leaving enough space to insert the stem. Tie the ends together and knot them twice.
4. Refer to "Stems" on page 25 to make a stem from the green wool 1¼" x 2" piece. Glue the stem into the opening of the eggplant.
5. Cut an X in the center of the calyx where indicated on the pattern. Gently place the calyx opening over the stem, pushing down any calyx pieces that come up as you pull the wool over the stem. Whipstitch (see page 28) the outer edges of the calyx to the eggplant with matching thread.
6. Add beads to the seams, if desired.

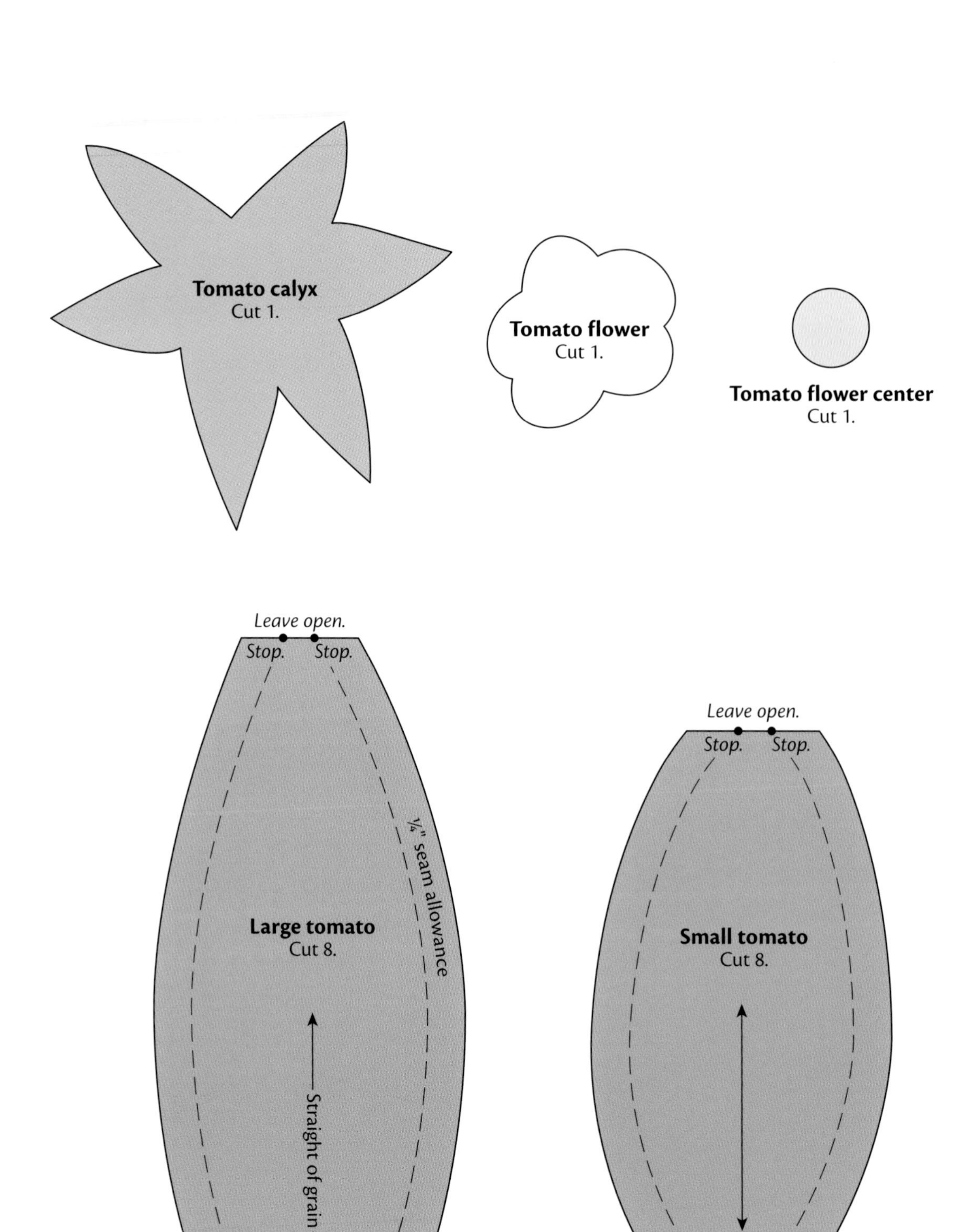
Tomato calyx
Cut 1.
Tomato flower
Cut 1.
Tomato flower center
Cut 1.
Leave open.
Stop.
Stop.
¼" seam allowance
Large tomato
Cut 8.
Straight of grain
Start.
Leave open.
Stop.
Stop.
Small tomato
Cut 8.
Start.

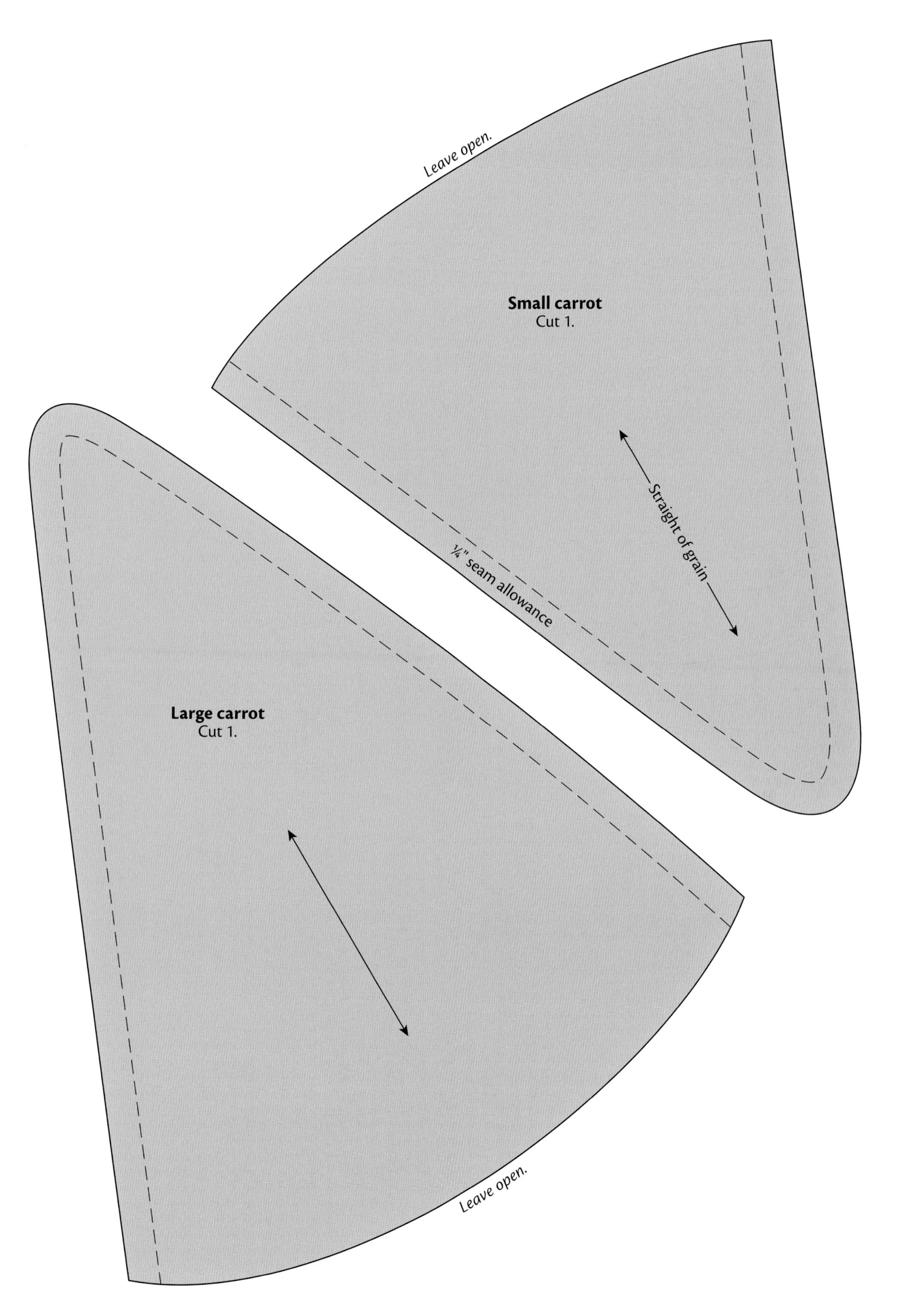
Leave open.
Small carrot
Cut 1.
Straight of grain
¼" seam allowance
Large carrot
Cut 1.
Leave open.

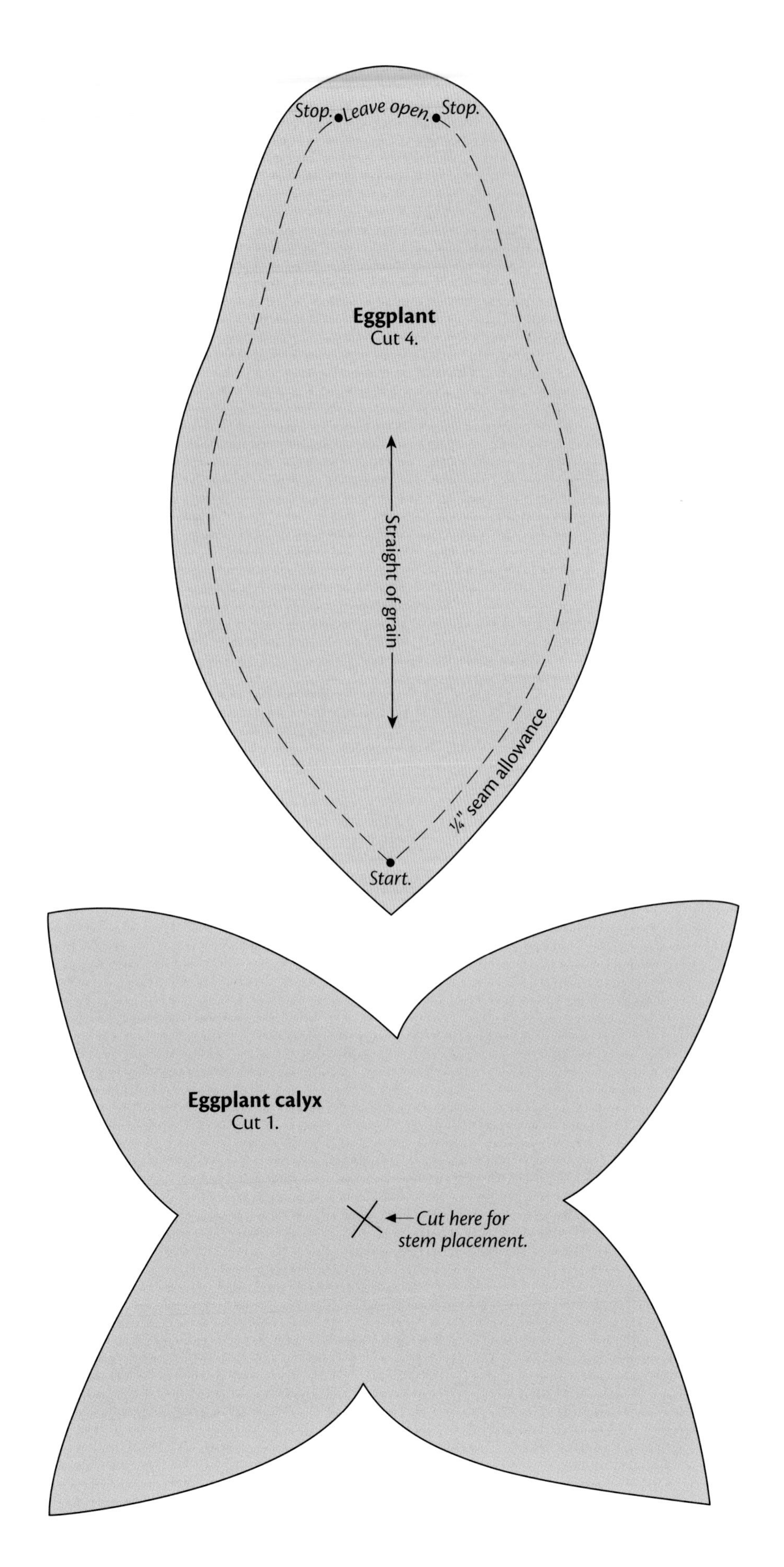
Stop.
Leave open.
Stop.
Eggplant
Cut 4.
Straight of grain
¼" seam allowance
Start.
Eggplant calyx
Cut 1.
Cut here for stem placement.

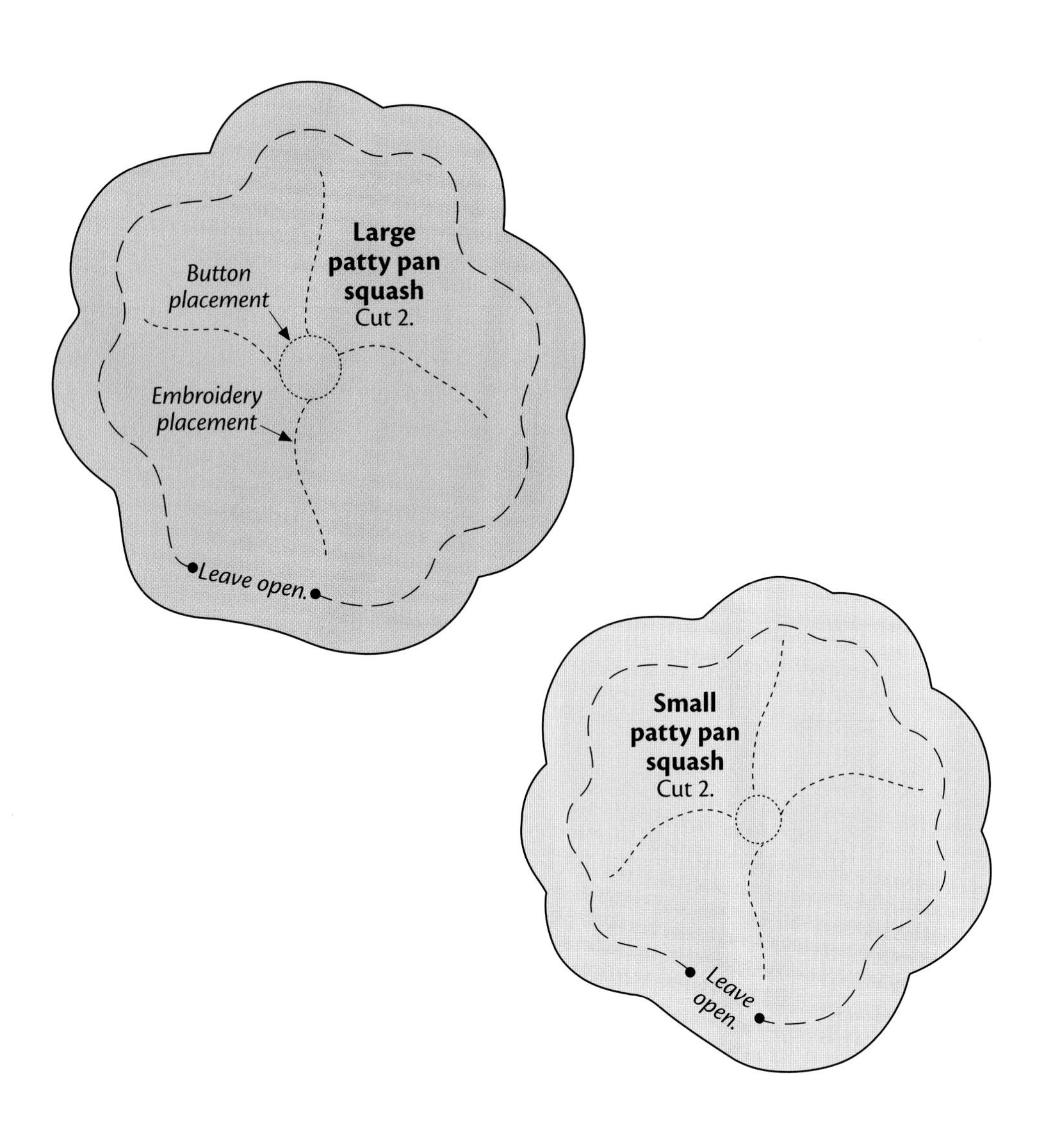
Large
patty pan
squash
Cut 2.
Button
placement
Embroidery
placement
Leave open.
Small
patty pan
squash
Cut 2.
Leave
open.

apron strings waist apron

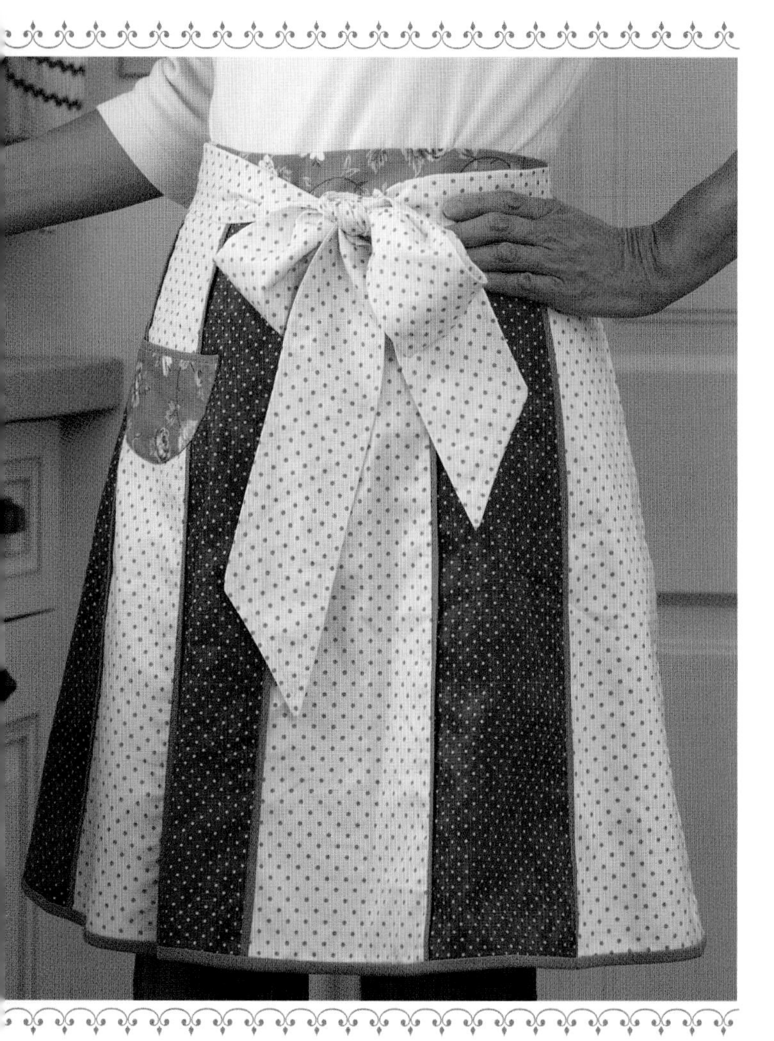

Designed and made by Janis Stob and Margaret Linderman.

Our extensive collection of vintage aprons is a constant source of joy and inspiration, whether for sewing or cooking. This one combines a few of our favorites that have a "let's wear this for a skirt" kind of attitude. Try tying one on and see what it does for your attitude!

—Janis and Margaret

MATERIALS

Yardages are based on 42"-wide fabrics unless otherwise noted.

1 yard of muslin for lining

1 yard of cream polka-dot fabric for apron front and ties

¾ yard of red polka-dot fabric for apron front

½ yard of coordinating fabric for pocket and waistband

½ yard of contrasting fabric for flanges and binding

⅛ yard of 22"-wide woven fusible interfacing (we used Form-Flex)

Freezer paper

CUTTING

All measurements include ¼"-wide seam allowances. The apron front and lining pieces will be cut after making the template.

From the cream polka-dot fabric, cut:
2 strips, 6½" x 42"

From the coordinating fabric for pocket and waistband, cut:
1 strip, 2½" x 42"; cut in half crosswise to make 2 pieces, 2½" x 21"
8" circle (We used a small dessert plate for our template.)

From the interfacing, cut:
1 piece, 2½" x 21"

CUTTING THE REMAINING PIECES

1. Cut out an 8" x 20" piece of freezer paper. Fold the paper in half to make a 4" x 20" piece. With the fold to the left, measure along the top edge 2¼" from the right edge and make a mark. Measure in ½" from the right edge along the bottom edge and make another mark. Draw a line to connect the two marks. With the paper still folded, cut on the line. Discard the two pieces that were cut away. The open folded piece is your apron panel template. Seam allowance is included in this template.

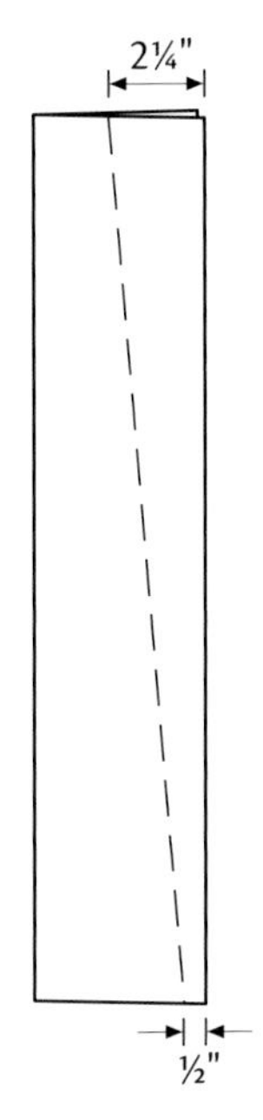

2. Use the apron panel template to cut four pieces from the remainder of the cream polka-dot fabric, three pieces from the red polka-dot fabric, and seven pieces from the muslin.
3. Refer to "Cutting Bias Strips" on page 27 to cut bias strips from the contrasting fabric. You will need six 1" x 20" pieces for the flanges, one 1" x 8" piece for the pocket trim, and one 2¼" x 50" strip for the binding.

ASSEMBLING THE APRON

1. Press each 1" x 20" flange piece in half lengthwise, wrong sides together. Sew to the right-hand edge of three cream polka-dot and three red polka-dot panels. You will have one cream polka-dot panel without a flange.

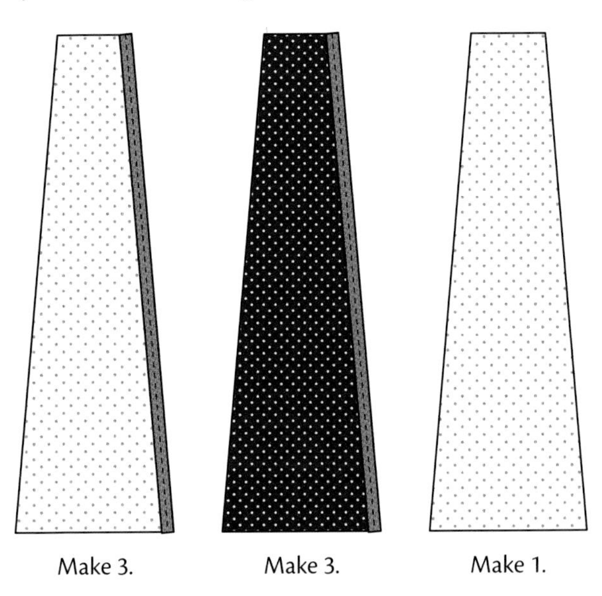

Make 3. Make 3. Make 1.

2. Lay out the front panels as shown, alternating colors and ending with the panel without a flange piece. Sew the panels right sides together along the flange edge in the established order. Press the flange away from the panel to which it was sewn.

FRESH TIP

When stitching the panels together, follow the stitching line from adding the flange. This will require you to flip the panels over after they are right sides together and sew from the bottom to the top of each piece, but there will be less chance that the previous stitching will show.

3. Sew the seven muslin lining panels together in the same manner as the front panels, omitting the flange detail. Press the seam allowances in the opposite direction as the front panels.
4. Place the front and lining right sides together, aligning the edges. Sew along the sides only, leaving the top and bottom edges open. Turn the apron right side out and press.
5. To make the ties, fold each cream polka-dot 6½" x 42" strip in half lengthwise, right sides together. Trim one end of each strip at a 45° angle. Sew along one long edge and angled end, leaving the straight end open. Turn the strips right side out and press.

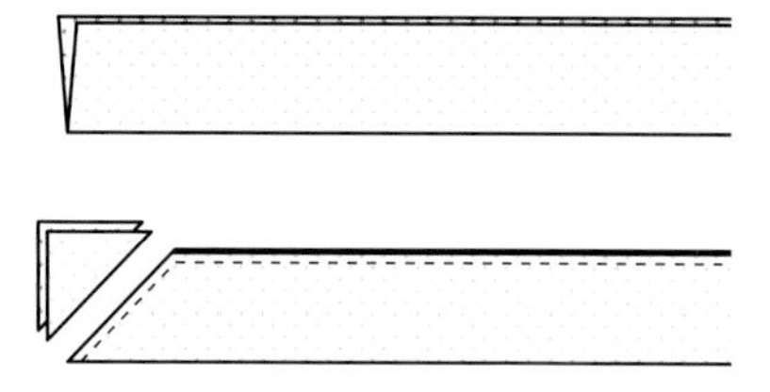

6. Topstitch ¼" from the finished edges of each tie.
7. Follow the manufacturer's instructions to fuse the interfacing piece to the wrong side of one of the coordinating fabric 2½" x 21" waistband pieces. With the right side of the fused piece face up, position the straight end of a tie piece on the end of the fused piece, making a small pleat at the straight end of the tie so there is about ½" of space between the sides of the tie and the sides of the waistband. Stitch the tie in place. Repeat on the opposite end of the waistband piece with the remaining tie.

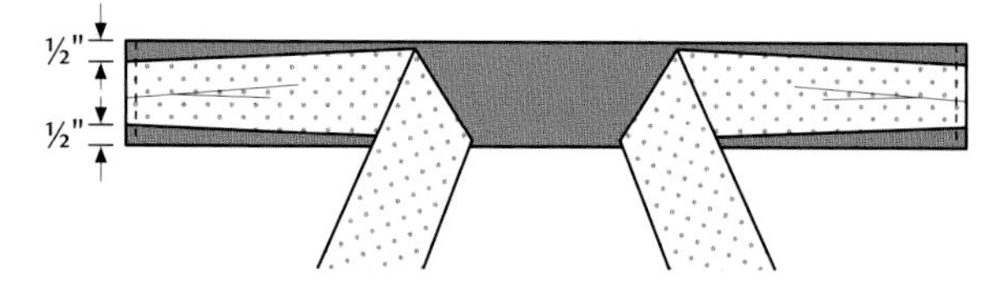

8. Fold the fused waistband piece in half crosswise to find the center; pin-mark the center point along one edge. Fold the apron in half lengthwise to find the center; pin-mark the center point at the top edge.
9. Pin the waistband piece to the front of the apron right sides together and center points aligned. Stitch the waistband in place along the top edge. Press the waistband up so that the raw edge is now at the top.

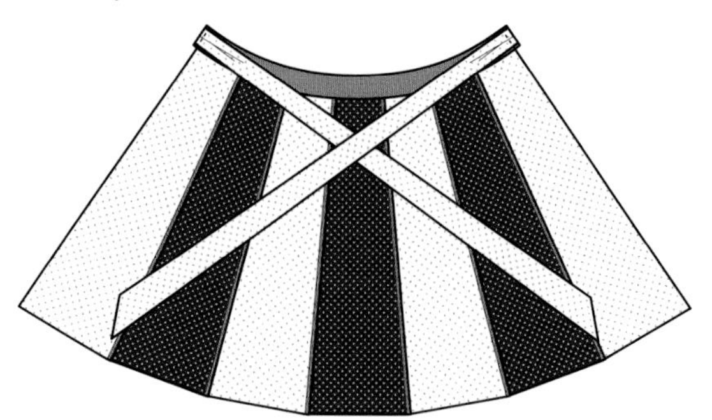

10. Press under ¼" along one long edge of the remaining coordinating 2½" x 21" piece. Place this piece over the stitched-on waistband piece, with the pressed-under edge at the bottom and the top edges aligned right sides together. The ties will be sandwiched between the layers. Stitch the pieces together along the ends and top edge.

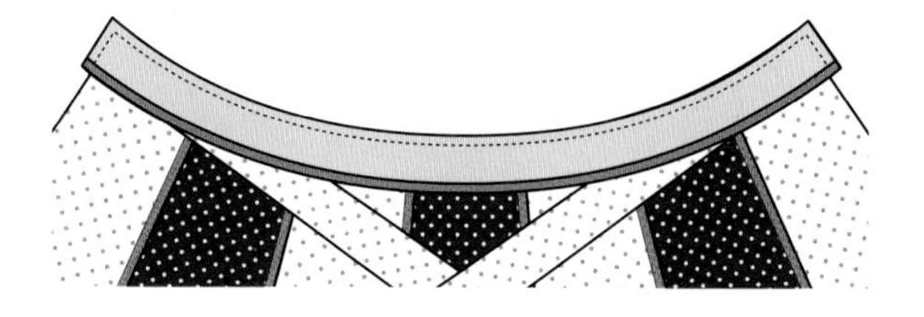

11. Turn the waistband to the right side and press, rolling the seam at the top of the waistband toward the lining side. Whipstitch the folded edge to the apron lining on the back side.

FINISHING THE APRON

1. Fold the pocket piece in half and cut along the fold. If necessary, trim the 1" x 8" bias piece to the same length as the cut edge. Fold the bias piece in half lengthwise, wrong sides together. With the raw edges aligned, place the bias piece along the cut edge of one of the pocket halves right sides together. Place the remaining pocket half over the first, right sides together, sandwiching the bias piece between the layers. Stitch all the way around, leaving a 1½" opening along one side for turning. Turn the pocket right side out and press the bias piece toward the top of the pocket. Whipstitch (see page 28) the opening closed.

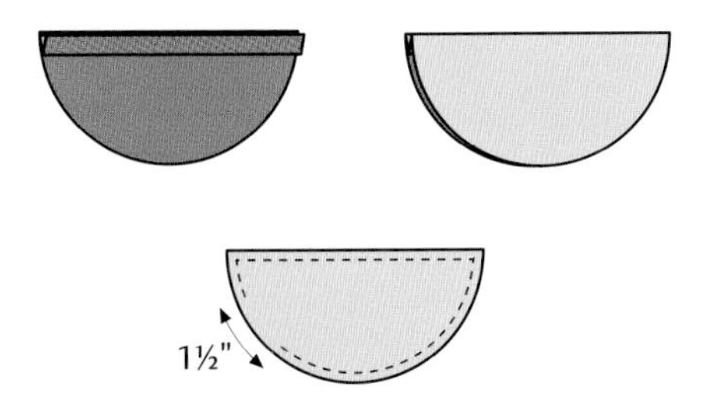

2. Center the pocket on the third panel (whichever side you prefer) of the apron front, approximately 3¾" from the bottom of the waistband. Stitch the pocket in place along the curved edge, backstitching at the beginning and end to reinforce the pocket corners.
3. Measure the bottom edge of the apron and cut the 2¼"-wide bias strip 1" longer than the measurement. Refer to "Binding" on page 22 to prepare the binding strip and stitch it to the front of the apron along the bottom edge. Press the binding away from the apron. Turn under the excess extending beyond each end ½" so it aligns with the sides of the apron. Fold the binding over the edge and whipstitch it to the apron lining.

a summer setting

Designed and created by Janis Stob and Margaret Linderman.

A table set with handmade cloth napkins and place mats is a special detail that really says, "Welcome and enjoy!" In our family this is how we learned (and in turn taught our children) to set a welcoming table for visiting family and friends.

—Janis and Margaret

Finished place mat size: 14½" x 19"
Finished napkin size: 18" x 18"

MATERIALS

Yardages are based on 42"-wide fabrics. Materials given are enough for 2 place mats and 2 napkins.

Place Mats

½ yard of green solid for pocket trim and binding

⅜ yard of red polka-dot print for center

⅜ yard of cream polka-dot print for sides

⅜ yard of orange print for pockets

⅝ yard of fabric for backing

⅝ yard of batting

Napkins

1⅜ yards of orange solid for front outer edges and back

⅝ yard of cream polka-dot print for center

CUTTING

All measurements include ¼"-wide seam allowances.

Place Mats

From the orange print, cut:
8 pieces, 5" x 6½"

From the red polka-dot fabric, cut
2 pieces, 10½" x 14½"

From the cream polka-dot fabric, cut:
4 pieces, 5" x 14½"

From the fabric for backing, cut:
2 pieces, 16" x 20"

From the batting, cut:
2 pieces, 16" x 20"

Napkins

From the orange solid, cut:
2 squares, 22" x 22"

From the cream polka-dot print, cut:
2 squares, 18" x 18"

MAKING THE PLACE MATS

1. Refer to "Cutting Bias Strips" on page 27 to cut four green 1" x 5" pieces for the trim. Press the pieces in half lengthwise, wrong sides together.
2. With right sides together and raw edges aligned, place a folded piece along the short edge of four orange 5" x 6½" pocket pieces. Place another orange 5" x 6½" pocket piece on top, wrong side up, aligning the edges. Stitch along the short edge with the bias trim. Turn the pieces so the right sides are out and press the trim away from the pockets.

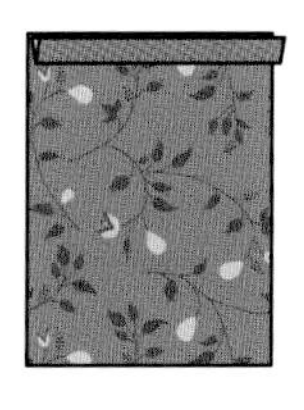
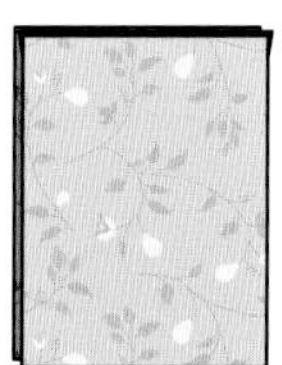
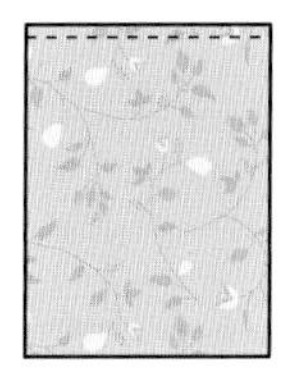
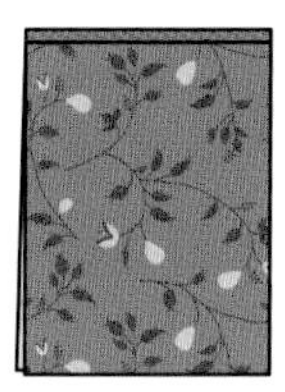

3. Lay a backing piece wrong side up on your work surface. Place a piece of batting on the top of the backing.
4. Center a red polka-dot piece over the batting as shown below. Quilt this section now, if desired. You don't have to quilt this section at all if you don't want to. If you don't quilt it, pin it in place so that it won't shift. Pin a pocket to the bottom left corner of the red polka-dot piece, aligning the sides and bottom edges.

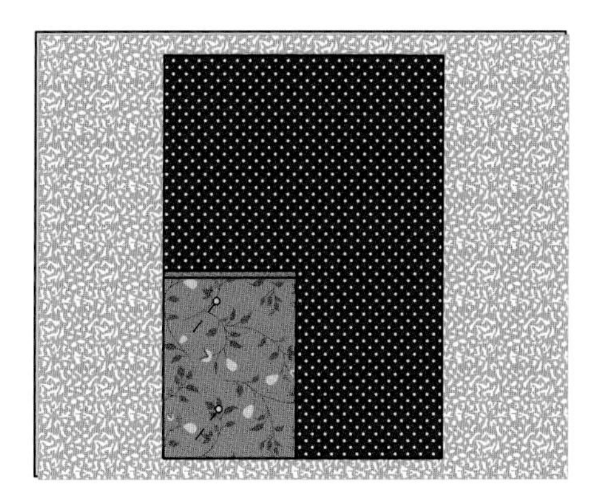

5. Place a cream polka-dot piece over the left side of the red polka-dot piece, right sides together and raw edges matching. The pocket will be sandwiched between the layers. Stitch 1/4" from the left raw edge of the cream piece through all the layers. Make sure you catch the pocket edges. Press the pocket and the cream fabric to the left.

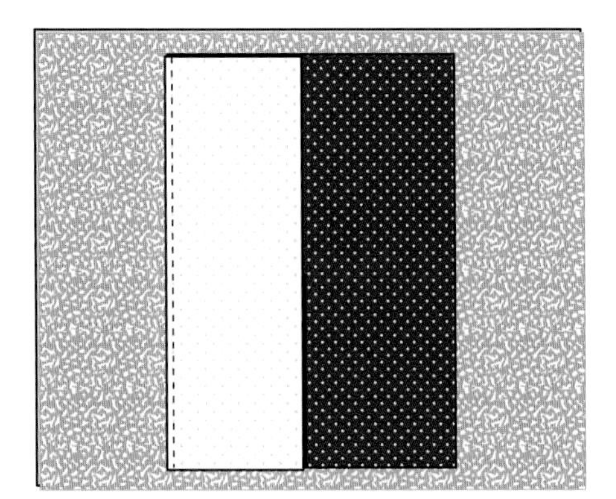

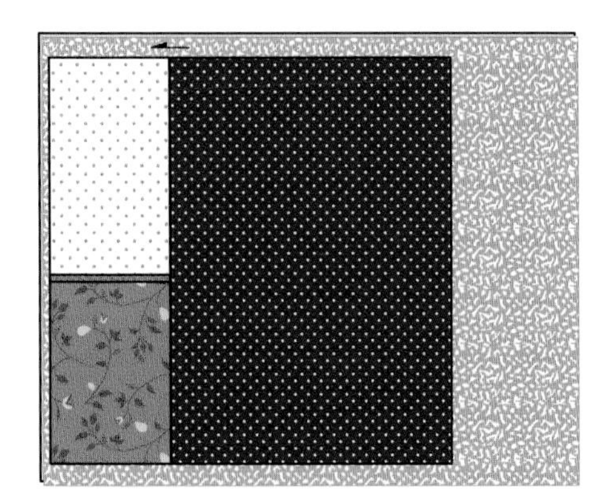

6. Repeat steps 5 and 6 on the bottom right side of the red polka-dot piece. Press the pocket and the cream piece to the right.

7. Trim the backing and batting even with the place mat top. Fold the piece in half lengthwise, right sides together. Curve the upper corners using a cereal bowl as a guide.

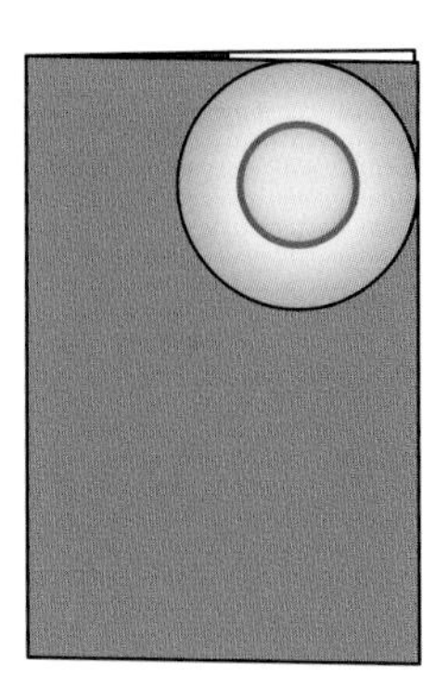

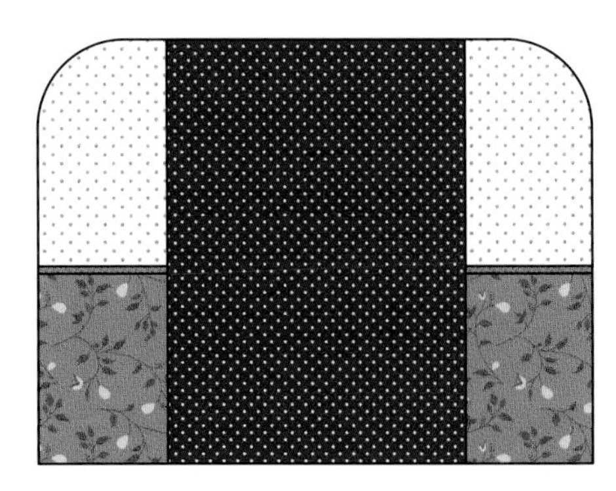

8. Repeat steps 3–9 to make one additional place mat.
9. Refer to "Cutting Bias Strips" to cut enough 2"-wide binding strips to equal 140" when pieced together. Refer to "Binding" on page 22 to bind the edges of each place mat.

MAKING THE NAPKINS

1. With wrong sides together, fold an orange solid square into quarters to make an 11" square. Fold a cream polka-dot square into quarters to make a 9" square.
2. Place the folded cream square on top of the orange square, lining up the folded corners. Place the 45° angle of your ruler across the top of the cream square, so that the ¼" line is at the point of the cream square. Cut along the edge of the ruler as shown.

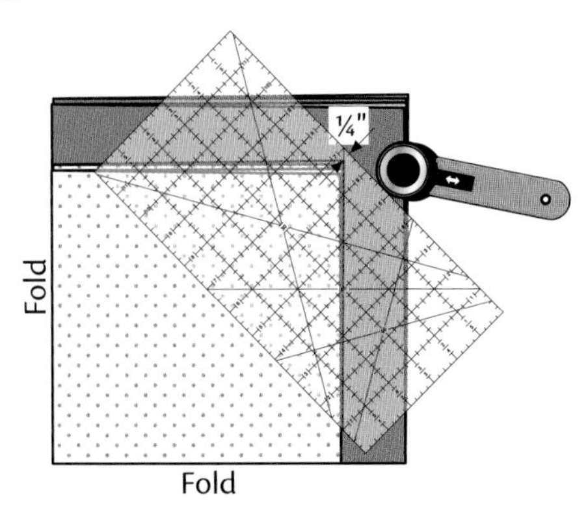

3. Set the cream square aside. Open up the orange square. The four corners should be cut at an angle. Make a mark ¼" from the point of each corner on the wrong side of the piece.

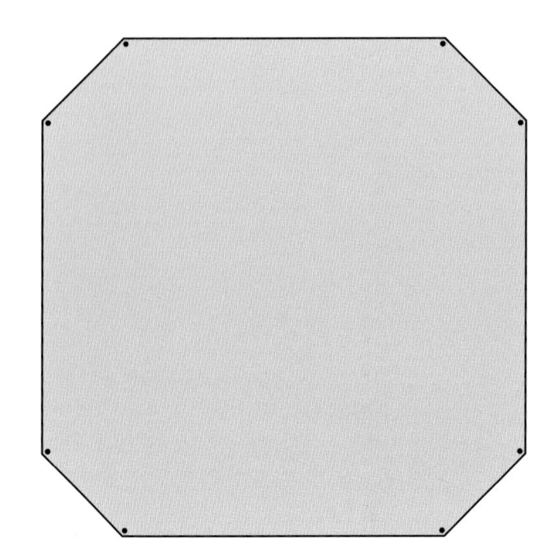

4. With right sides together, fold one of the angled corners in half, matching the outer edge. Stitch from the marked point to the fold, backstitching at the beginning and end. This will miter the corner. Repeat for each corner.

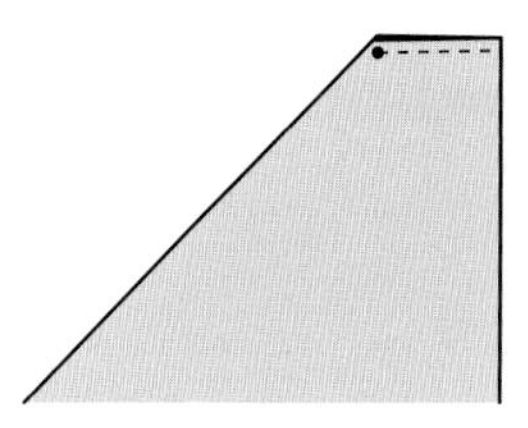

5. Turn the piece to the right side and press it flat. Press under the raw edges ¼".

6. Place the cream square in the opening of the orange square. Tuck the raw edges of the cream square under the pressed-under edges of the orange square. Pin around the opening. Topstitch ⅛" away from the opening along the pressed-under edges.

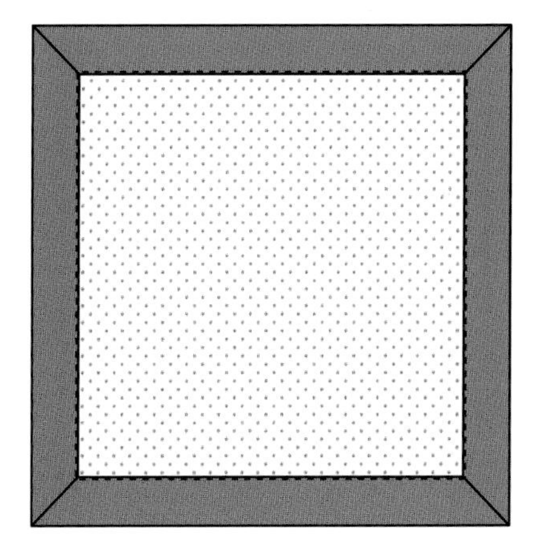

7. Repeat steps 1–6 to make one additional napkin.
8. Place your silverware in the right pockets of your place mats and your napkins in the left pockets.

from grandma's kitchen

Designed and made by Janis Stob and Margaret Linderman.

A tattered group of cherished recipes are the legacy we chase around our kitchens. To celebrate a wedding in the family, we decided to create a set of recipes to pass on, and of course we needed a fun holder in which to keep them! This is what we came up with to keep them from getting lost or from flying around!

—Janis and Margaret

Finished recipe holder size: 5" x 6"

MATERIALS

¼ yard of fabric for outer cover

¼ yard of coordinating fabric for inner cover

8" x 16" piece of double-sided fusible stiff interfacing (we used fast2fuse)

2 yards of rickrack or flat trim (optional)

Pinking blade for rotary cutter

1 package of 4"x 6" index cards

Heavy-duty single-hole punch

2 loose-leaf rings, 2" diameter

CUTTING

From *each* of the outer and inner cover fabrics and the interfacing, cut:
2 squares, 8" x 8"

MAKING THE RECIPE HOLDER

1. Lay one outer cover piece wrong side up on your ironing board. Place a piece of the interfacing over it. Lay an inner-cover piece right side up over the interfacing. Follow the manufacturer's instructions to fuse the layers together. Repeat with the remaining pieces.
2. Trim each fused piece from step 1 to approximately 5" x 6" using the pinking blade on your rotary cutter.
3. Topstitch 1/8" from the edges of each piece, or stitch the rickrack or trim to the outer cover, placing it about 1/4" in from the edges.
4. Measure 3/4" in and 1/2" down from the top corners of each piece and make a mark. Punch a hole at these two points. Measure, mark, and punch the index cards in the same manner.
5. Place the recipe-cover pieces and cards onto the hinged rings so that the outer covers are on the outside. Write recipes onto the index cards or print them onto paper, and then glue or stitch them onto the index cards.

Here is one of our favorite recipes to get you started! In addition to being positively scrumptious, this recipe is good for when you're baking with children. The cookies are good without anything extra, but they're especially good with a little sanding sugar sprinkled on them before they're baked or with frosting added to them after they cool.

MARGARET'S SHORTBREAD HEAVENLY COOKIES

1/2 pound (2 sticks) butter, softened

1/2 cup plus 1 tablespoon packed brown sugar

1 tablespoon vanilla

2 cups flour

Preheat oven to 275°. In a large mixing bowl, cream together the butter, brown sugar, and vanilla. Stir in the flour, 1/2 cup at a time using a wooden spoon. Divide the dough into two balls and knead until smooth. Roll out dough 1/8" to 1/4" thick. Cut the dough into shapes with cookie cutters. Place the shapes on a cookie sheet and bake just until light brown on the bottom. Cool on wire rack.

Chocolat et Crème

It's all about the fabric, right? This grouping was created all around this chocolate floral fabric from one of Fig Tree Quilts recent fabric collections. It is one of my all-time favorite prints, and I can't count how many different projects I have created using it. It just embodies that fresh vintage feel that I'm always after. Here the quilt, the album, the folders, and the pear all work together to bring about elements of stylish and charming decoration to your home!

chocolat et crème quilt

Inspired by one of my all-time favorite floral fabrics, this quilt flowed naturally from the soft color palette of the fabric itself. So, start with the floral that inspires you, add a few coordinating fabrics, and you will be well on your way to creating your own Creme masterpiece.

—Joanna

Finished quilt size: 67" x 67" Finished block size: 14" x 14"

MATERIALS

Yardages are based on 42"-wide fabrics.

3 yards of cream solid for background

1½ yards of small-scale cream print for block centers and outer border

1 yard of green polka-dot fabric for block star points

1 yard of chocolate brown floral for large star points and inner border

⅝ yard of fabric for binding

4 yards of fabric for backing

73" x 73" piece of batting

CUTTING

All measurements include ¼"-wide seam allowances.

From the cream solid for background, cut:

12 strips, 4" x 42"; crosscut into:
- 36 squares, 4" x 4"
- 36 pieces, 4" x 7½"

2 strips, 7½" x 42"; crosscut into 4 pieces, 7½" x 14½"

4 strips, 7½" x 42"; crosscut *each* strip into:
- 1 piece, 7½" x 21½" (4 total)
- 1 piece, 7½" x 14½" (4 total)

From the small-scale cream print, cut:

2 strips, 7½" x 42"; crosscut into 9 squares, 7½" x 7½"

8 strips, 4" x 42"

From the green polka-dot fabric, cut:

8 strips, 4" x 42"; crosscut into 72 squares, 4" x 4"

From the chocolate brown floral, cut:

2 strips, 7½" x 42"; crosscut into 8 squares, 7½" x 7½"

6 strips, 2½" x 42"

From the fabric for binding, cut:

7 strips, 2¼" x 42"

Designed and sewn by Joanna Figueroa; quilted by Diana Johnson.

PIECING THE BLOCKS

1. Press the green squares in half diagonally, right sides together.
2. Refer to "Triangle Units" on page 17 to join a pressed green square to one end of a cream 4" x 7½" piece, orienting and sewing on the fold line as shown. Repeat on the opposite end of the cream piece. Repeat to make a total of 36 flying-geese units.

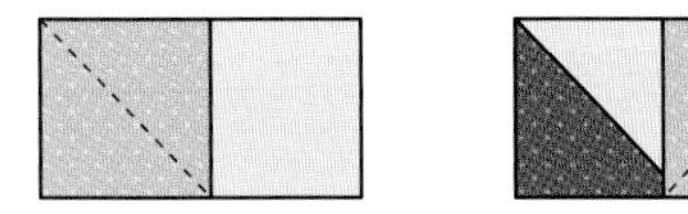

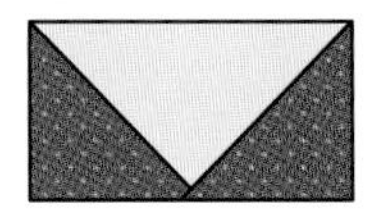

Make 36.

3. Sew a flying-geese unit to the sides of a small-scale cream print 7½" square. Press the seam allowances toward the square. Join a cream 4" square to the ends of two additional flying-geese units. Press the seam allowances toward the squares. Sew these units to the top and bottom of the previous unit. Press the seam allowances away from the center square. Repeat to make a total of nine blocks.

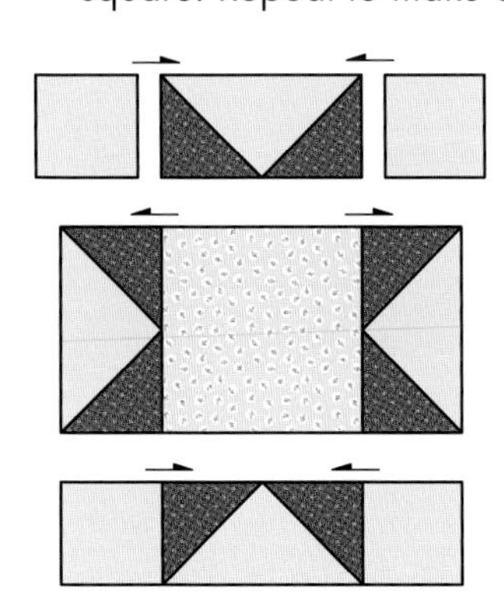

Make 9.

> **FRESH TIP**
>
> Whenever you're sewing together pieces with points, like these stars, always sew with the "point" piece on top. As you're sewing, you'll be able to see the point and make slight adjustments to your seam line so that you stitch right above the tip and have perfect points. Small adjustments in or out on your sewing line will not affect your block and it will help you achieve crisp star points every time.

ASSEMBLING THE QUILT TOP

1. Press the chocolate floral 7½" squares in half diagonally, right sides together. Repeat step 2 of "Piecing the Blocks" to make four flying-geese units with the folded chocolate floral squares and four cream 7½" x 14½" pieces.
2. Sew a flying-geese unit to one side of four blocks as shown. Press the seam allowances toward the blocks.

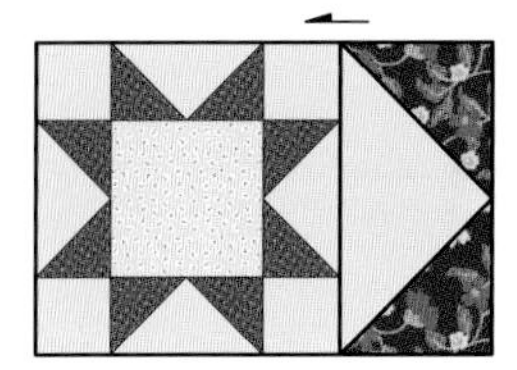

Make 4.

3. Join a cream 7½" x 14½" piece to the left edge of two blocks and then to the right edge of two blocks. Press the seam allowance toward the cream piece. Sew a cream 7½" x 21½" piece to the top of these units. Press the seam allowances toward the cream pieces.

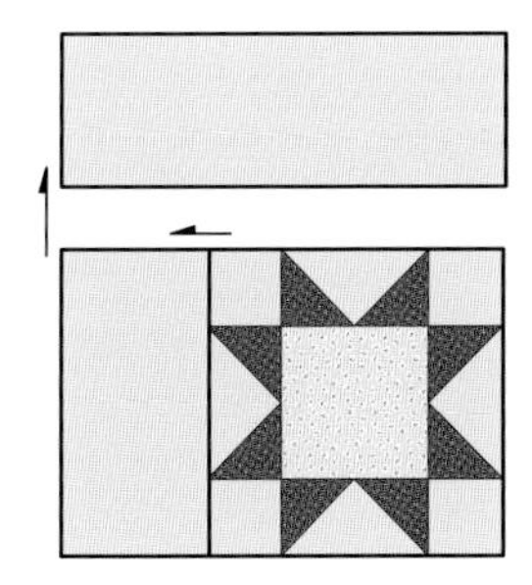
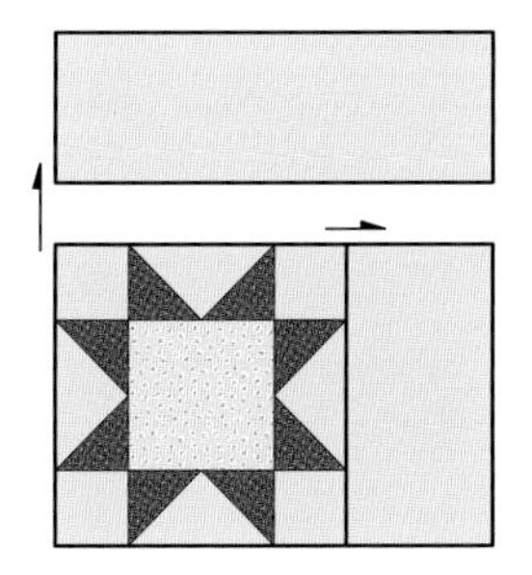

Make 2 of each.

4. Arrange the units from steps 2 and 3 and the remaining block into three vertical rows. Sew the units in each row together. Press the seam allowances as indicated. Sew the rows together. Press the seam allowances in one direction.

5. Refer to "Adding Borders" on page 20 to add the chocolate floral 2½"-wide inner-border strips to the quilt top, piecing as necessary. Repeat with the small-scale cream print 4"-wide strips for the outer border.

FINISHING THE QUILT

Refer to "Finishing Techniques" on page 21 for detailed instructions.

1. Layer the quilt top with batting and backing; baste.
2. Quilt as desired. Diana created dramatic wreaths and feathers. This type of heirloom quilting really adds to the vintage flavor of a quilt.
3. Bind the quilt edges with the 2¼"-wide binding strips.

la grande poire

Designed and sewn by Jackie Cate.

Pears are one of the most lovely fruits—from the shapes to the colors and the variety. I started making pear pincushions as one of my first designs. I bought some tiny Seckel pears at the farmers' market and was intrigued by their rich crimson and gold colors. Also, our neighbors have a beautiful pear tree that I can see from my studio. Those pears are lovely and big and green. This *belle grande poire* represents a mixture of them all.

—Jackie

MATERIALS

3 pieces, 6" x 9", of assorted coordinating fabrics

3" x 6" piece of green felted wool for rolled stem

4 fat eighths of assorted green felted wool fabrics for leaves

Embroidery floss in colors to match pear and leaves

Size 10 embroidery needle

Size 11 seed beads (optional)

Size 11 straw needle (optional)

6" of florist wire (optional)

8"-tall unfinished wood candlestick

Cream craft paint

Small paintbrush

Fine-grit sandpaper (optional)

Tacky glue (if leaves are wired)

Hot glue gun and glue stick

General pincushion supplies (see page 24)

ASSEMBLING THE PINCUSHION

Refer to "Basic Pincushion Instructions" on page 24.

1. Use the patterns at right to make freezer-paper templates for the pear and pear leaves. Cut out each of the pear pieces from a different fabric. Mark the starting and stopping points on the wrong side of each piece. Cut out the leaves from the assorted green fat eighths.
2. With right sides together, sew the pear pieces together side by side along the *left side only*, starting and stopping where indicated. Stitch the end pieces together to form the shape, leaving an openingat the top. Turn the piece right side out and stuff it. This one takes a lot of stuffing and patience, so take your time.

3. Refer to "Stems" on page 25 to create a rolled stem from the 3" x 6" piece of green wool, rolling along the 6" side. Use the hand-quiting thread to make a running stitch around the opening at the top, leaving a 4" tail on both ends. Insert the stem into the opening, applying some glue to hold it in place. Pull the thread ends to tightly gather the fabric around the stem. Knot the thread ends twice and cut off the excess thread.
4. Use the size 10 embroidery needle and three strands of floss that match the pear fabrics to feather stitch (see page 28) along the seams. After the feather stitches have been created, if desired, add a bead to the end of each "feather" to resemble buds or berries.
5. Refer to "Leaves" on page 26 to sew two large leaf shapes together, adding the florist wire between the shapes if desired. Stitch the leaf to the pear near the stem.
6. Paint the candlestick with the cream paint. Add additional coats as needed to achieve the desired color. If you want more of a distressed, antique look, lightly sand the candlestick in various places after the paint has dried completely.
7. Hot glue the remaining large leaves to the top of the candlestick so they drape over the sides. Hot glue the small leaves over the large leaves.
8. Hot glue the bottom of the pear to the top of the candlestick.

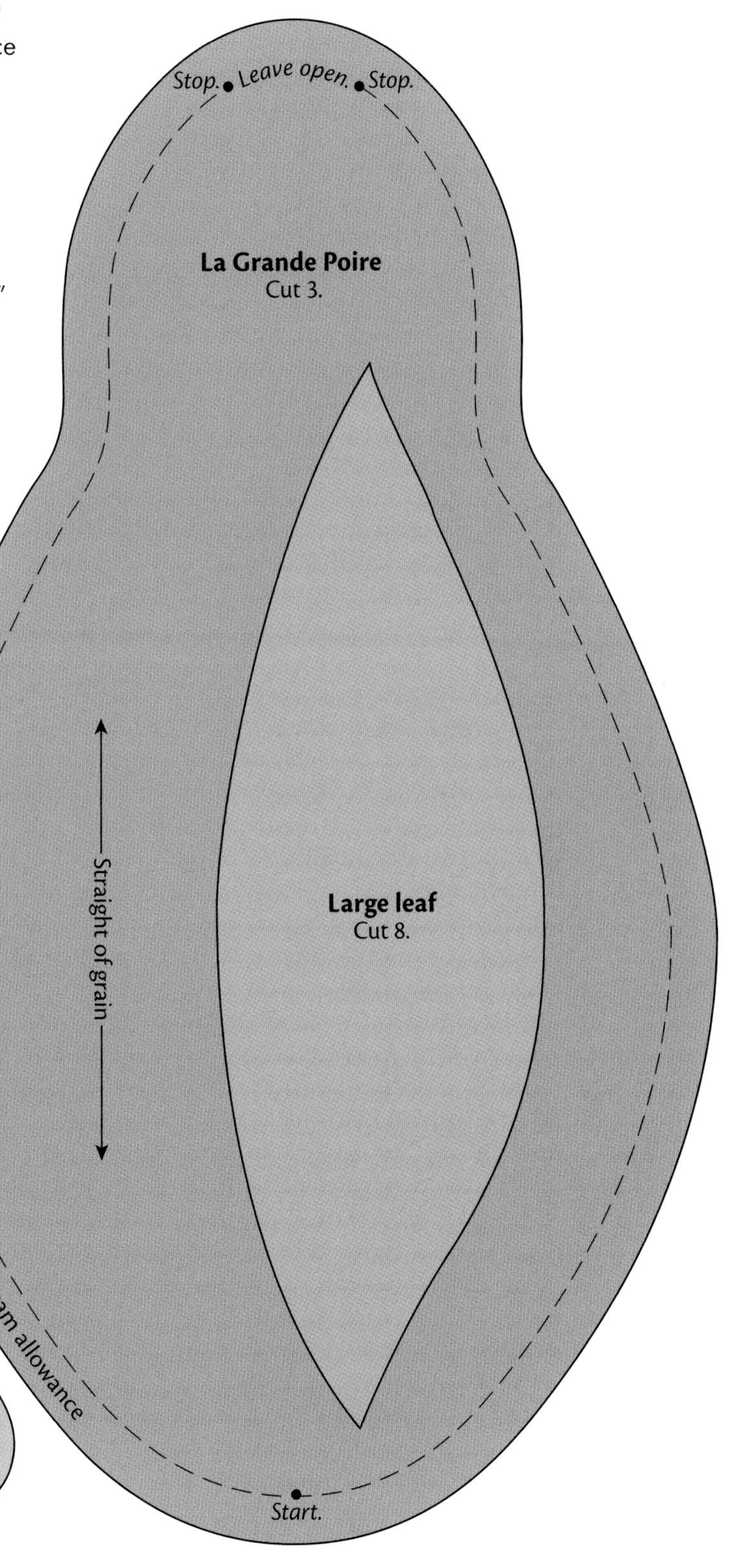

Small leaf
Cut 6.

le journal de paris

Designed and created by Janis Stob and Margaret Linderman.

Paris in the summer—what could be more worth recording in your own personalized album? All of the textures and textiles of a spectacular trip were the inspiration for creating this photo album cover. Of course your inspiration could be anything, a cherished vacation, your kids, or the record of a wonderful year!

—Janis and Margaret

Finished size: To fit a photo album 10¾" x 11¾" with a 2"-wide spine

MATERIALS

Yardages are based on 42"-wide fabrics.

⅜ yard of sage solid for outer cover (and flaps)

⅝ yard sage-and-cream print for flanges and inner cover

⅜ yard of neutral-colored flannel (this will be used in place of batting)

¼ yard of cream solid for appliqué background and frame backing

⅛ yard of large-scale floral print for appliqué frame

3" x 10" piece of felted wool to match large-scale floral print for Paris appliqué

Wool floss to match appliqué fabric

CUTTING

All measurements include ¼"-wide seam allowances.

From the cream solid, cut:

2 pieces, 5" x 5½"

1 piece, 7½" x 8½"

From the large-scale floral print, cut:

2 pieces, 2" x 5"

2 pieces, 1¾" x 8½"

From *each* of the outer cover, inner cover, and flannel fabrics, cut:

1 piece, 12¼" x 37"

From the remainder of the sage-and-cream print, cut:

2 pieces, 1" x 24¾"

2 pieces, 1¼" x 18½"

MAKING THE APPLIQUÉD PIECE

1. Refer to "Appliqué" on page 17 and use the pattern on page 92 to cut out the appliqué from the wool fabric.
2. Lay the cream 5" x 5½" pieces right sides up. Position the appliqué on the pieces at a slight angle and appliqué it in place with the wool floss, stitching through both layers of the cream fabric.
3. Sew the floral 2" x 5" pieces to the sides of the appliquéd piece. Press the seam allowances toward the strips. Sew the floral 1¾" x 8½" pieces to the top and bottom of the appliquéd piece. Press the seam allowances toward the strips.

4. Place the cream 7½" x 8½" piece and the appliquéd piece right sides together. Stitch completely around the piece. Trim the corners. Cut a slit about 3" long in the cream backing piece only and turn the piece right side out. Push out the corners, and press.

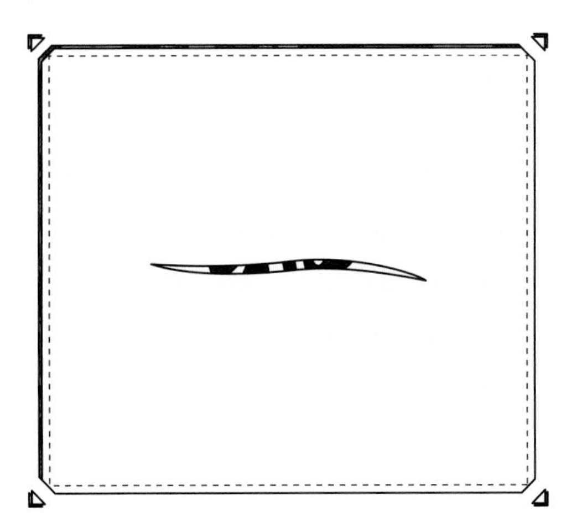

ASSEMBLING THE COVER

1. Place the flannel piece on your work surface. Layer the outer-cover piece over it, right side up. Place the inner-cover piece over the outer-cover piece, wrong side up. Make sure all the edges are aligned. Stitch the short edges together. Turn the piece right side out. Fold the piece in half crosswise so the finished ends meet; pin mark the top and bottom edges at the fold to mark the center.
2. Fold the 1" x 24¾" flange strips in half lengthwise, right sides together, and stitch along the ends. Turn the pieces right side out and press. Fold each strip in half crosswise to find the center and mark it with a pin.
3. Place the cover piece from step 1 on your work surface with the outer-cover fabric face up. With raw edges and centers aligned, pin a flange to the top and bottom edges.

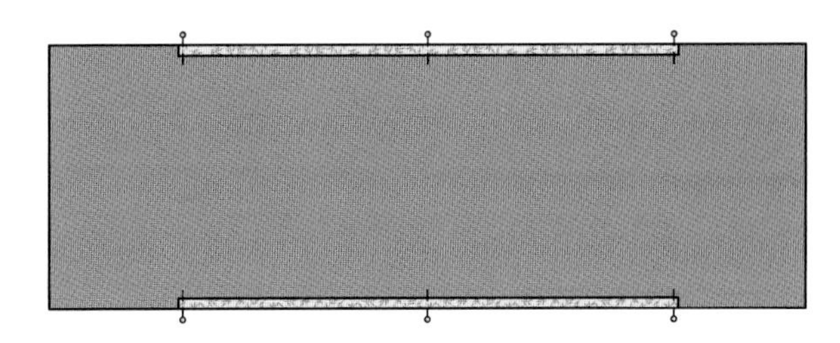

4. Measure in 12" from each side of the cover and place a pin at the top and bottom edges. Bring the sides of the cover to the pin marks to create a 6"-deep flap (the lining side will be visible); pin the flaps in place along the top and bottom edges.

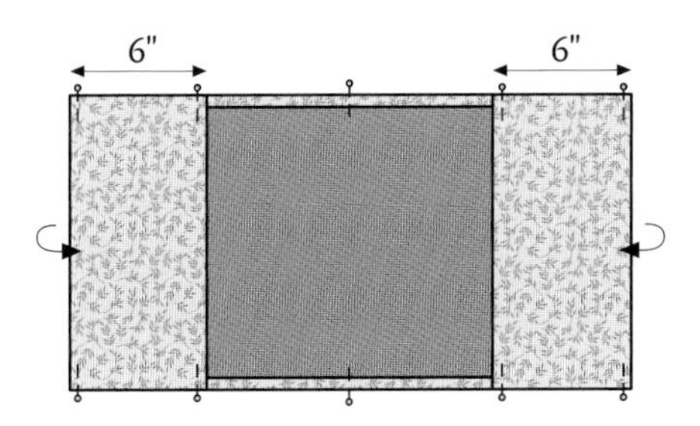

5. Press under 1/4" on the ends and one long edge of each inner fabric 1 1/4" x 18 1/2" facing piece. With right sides together, center the pieces along the top and bottom edges of the cover. Stitch across the top and bottom edges. Carefully trim the corners at an angle.

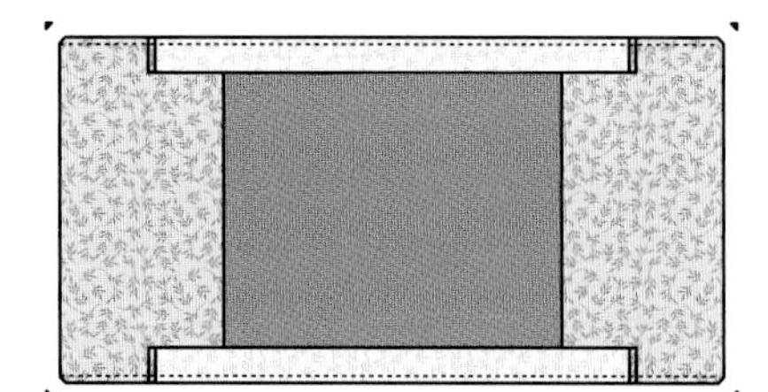

6. Wrap the facing pieces over the stitched edges and hand whipstitch (see page 28) the folded edges to the inner cover. Turn the cover to the right side and press, pressing the flanges out toward the edges.

7. Position the appliqué piece on the front of the cover where desired and whipstitch it in place around the outer edges. Machine stitch, or use a hand running stitch (see page 28) to stitch around the inside of the frame edges, stitching through all the layers, and being careful not to stitch through the flaps.

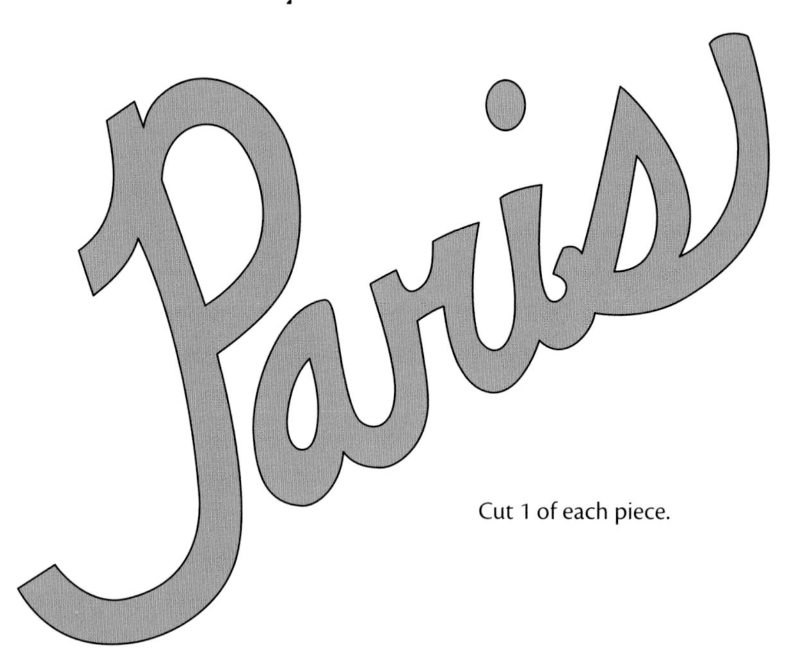

Cut 1 of each piece.

fleurette file folders

Designed and created by Janis Stob and Margaret Linderman.

We love all things floral and all things that organize! File folders have become such a mainstay of our lives that we thought it would be nice if we could personalize them with all of our favorite fabrics. These couldn't be easier—you won't be able to make just one!

—Janis and Margaret

Finished folder size: 9½" x 11⅝"

MATERIALS

1 fat quarter of large-scale floral print for folder outside

1 fat quarter of small-scale floral print for folder inside

¾ yard of lightweight paper-backed fusible transfer web (we used HeatnBond Lite)

Thread to match large-scale floral print

Letter-size manila file folder

MAKING THE FILE FOLDER

1. Open up the manila file folder and lay it on the paper side of the fusible web. Trace around the folder. Turn the folder over and repeat to trace one additional shape onto the web, leaving space between each shape. Roughly cut around the shapes.
2. Follow the manufacturer's instructions to fuse one shape to the wrong side of each of the fabrics, making sure to fuse the inside shape to the inside fabric, and the outside shape to the outside fabric. Cut out the shapes on the drawn lines. Remove the paper backing from each shape.
3. Fuse the small-scale floral shape to the inside of the file folder and the large-scale floral shape to the outside of the file folder.
4. Set your sewing machine for a zigzag stitch with stitches fairly close together but not as close together as a satin stitch. Using thread that matches the outside fabric in the needle and bobbin, stitch around the outside edges of the file folder. The best way to ensure a good finish is to go around the file folder at least twice using a wider and more closely spaced stitch each subsequent round than you did for the previous round. Guide the folder with both hands and stitch slowly around corners.

An English Boudoir

This collection was inspired by the feminine and romantic side in all of us. Even if we are not the overtly feminine and flowery type, there is a part of each of us that longs for small touches of romance, for serenity, and for a retreat from the daily routine. The projects in this grouping are a few things that we hope might create that kind of space for you. A soft quilt, an enchanting cubby holder, a few sweet pillows or sachets, and a journal . . . let the dreaming take you somewhere far away, if even for just a little bit!

lady charlotte quilt

This romantic quilt started with the Burgoyne Surrounded quilt block. I did a little bit of research on where the name came from and found it was a reference to the defeat and surrender of the English General Burgoyne in the American Revolution. Not very romantic in my mind! A little more research and I discovered that earlier in his life Burgoyne had eloped with Lady Charlotte—much more romantic and quite appropriate for the name of this delicate, romantic quilt!

—Denise

Finished quilt size: 87" x 87" Finished block size: 17" x 17"

MATERIALS

Yardages are based on 42"-wide fabrics.

5 yards of cream print for block background and inner border

1 7/8 yards of aqua large-scale floral for outer border

1 1/3 yards of chocolate brown print for blocks

1 yard of caramel print for middle border

1/2 yard of aqua small-scale floral for blocks

2/3 yard of fabric for binding

8 1/2 yards of fabric for backing

93" x 93" piece of batting

CUTTING

All measurements include 1/4"-wide seam allowances.

From the aqua small-scale floral, cut:
4 strips, 3 1/2" x 42"

From the cream print, cut:
14 strips, 1 1/2" x 42". Set aside 12 strips; crosscut the remaining 2 strips into 36 squares, 1 1/2" x 1 1/2"

33 strips, 3 1/2" x 42". Set aside 12 strips; crosscut the remaining strips into:
- 36 pieces, 3 1/2" x 7 1/2"
- 24 pieces, 3 1/2" x 17 1/2"
- 2 pieces, 3 1/2" x 20"
- 4 strips, 7 1/2" x 42"

From the chocolate brown print, cut:
17 strips, 1 1/2" x 42"

3 strips, 3 1/2" x 42"; cut 1 strip in half crosswise

1 piece, 1 1/2" x 20"

From the caramel print, cut:
8 strips, 3 1/2" x 42"

From the aqua large-scale floral, cut:
9 strips, 6 1/2" x 42"

From the fabric for binding, cut:
9 strips, 2 1/4" x 42"

Designed and sewn by Denise Sheehan; quilted by Diana Johnson.

PIECING THE BLOCKS

1. Join two aqua 3½" x 42" strips and one cream 1½" x 42" strip as shown to make strip set A. Repeat to make a total of two strip sets. Press the seam allowances toward the aqua strips. Crosscut the strip set into 18 segments, 3½" wide.

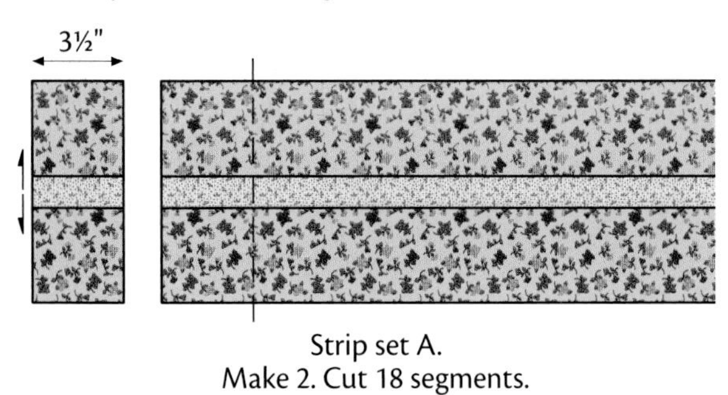

Strip set A.
Make 2. Cut 18 segments.

2. Join two cream 3½" x 42" strips and one brown 1½" x 42" strip as shown to make strip set B. Press the seam allowances toward the brown strip. Crosscut the strip set into nine segments, 1½" wide.

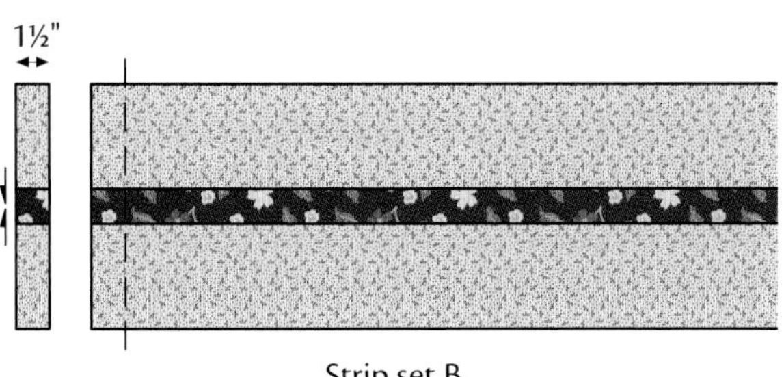

Strip set B.
Make 1. Cut 9 segments.

3. Sew two A segments and one B segment together to make a block center unit. Press the seam allowances toward the A segments. Repeat to make a total of nine units.

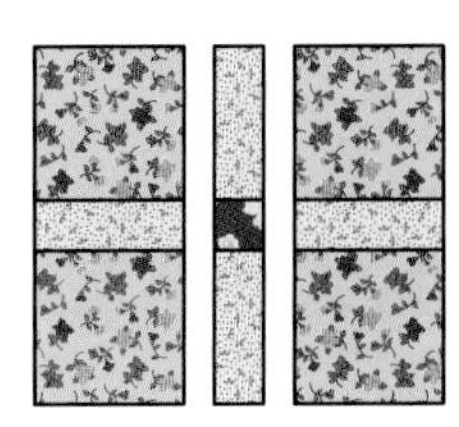

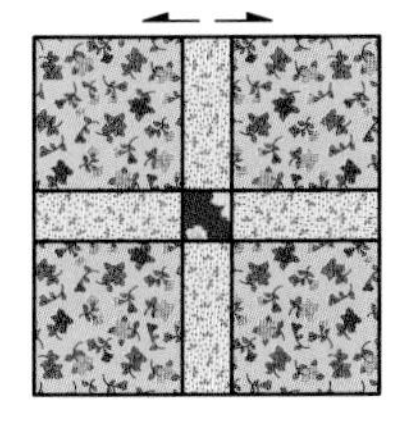

Make 9.

4. Join two brown 1½" x 42" strips and one cream 1½" x 42" strip as shown to make strip set C. Repeat to make a total of four strip sets. Press the seam allowances toward the brown strips. Crosscut the strip sets into 88 segments, 1½" wide.

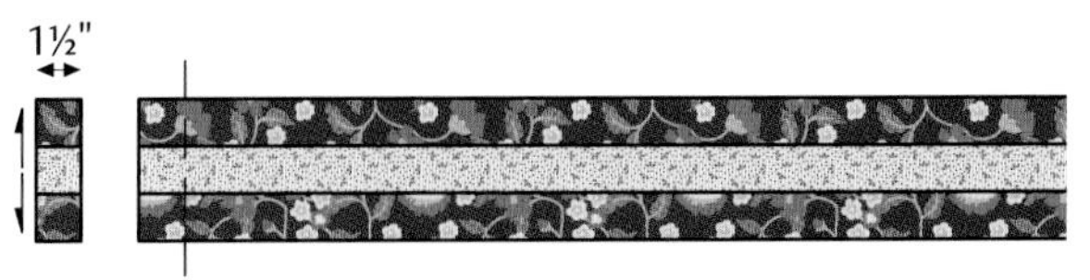

Strip set C.
Make 4. Cut 88 segments.

5. Join two cream 1½" x 42" strips and one brown 1½" x 42" strip as shown to make strip set D. Repeat to make a total of three strip sets. Press the seam allowances toward the brown strips. Crosscut the strip sets into 68 segments, 1½" wide.

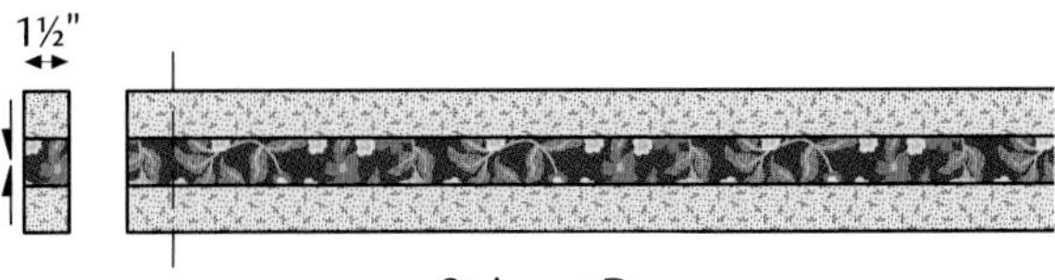

Strip set D.
Make 3. Cut 68 segments.

6. Sew two C segments and one D segment together to make a brown nine-patch unit. Repeat to make a total of 36 units. Sew two D segments and one C segment together to make a cream nine-patch unit. Repeat to make a total of 16 units. Set the cream units aside for the sashing.

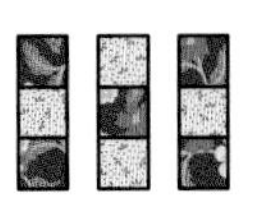

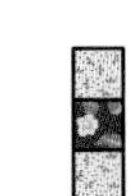

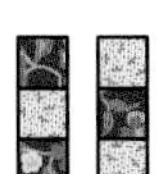

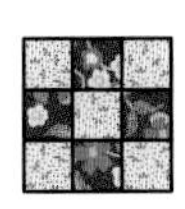

Make 36. Make 16.

7. Sew a cream 3½" x 7½" piece to the sides of each center unit from step 3. Press the seam allowances toward the cream pieces. Join a brown nine-patch unit to the ends of each of the remaining cream 3½" x 7½" pieces. Press the seam allowances toward the cream pieces. Add these units to the top and bottom of each center unit. Press the seam allowances toward the center units.

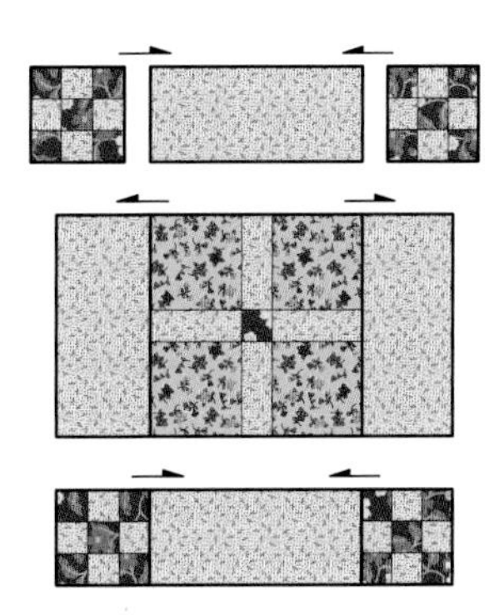

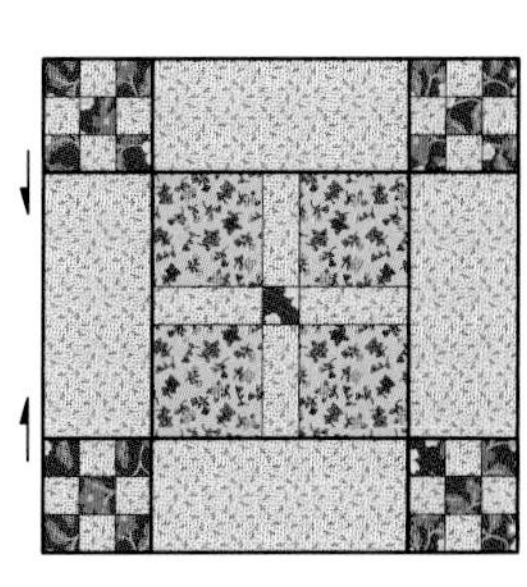

Make 9.

8. Join a cream 3½" x 42" strip to a brown 3½" x 42" strip to make strip set E. Repeat with one cream and one brown 3½" x 20" strip to make a half-strip set. Press the seam allowances toward the cream strips. Crosscut the strip sets into 36 segments, 1½" wide.

Strip set E.
Make 1½. Cut 36 segments.

9. Sew an E segment to opposite sides of a cream 1½" square. Press the seam allowances toward the E segments. Repeat to make a total of 18 units.

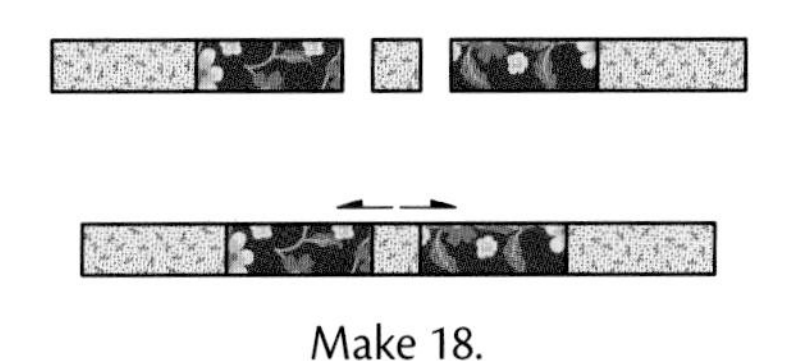

Make 18.

10. Join one brown 1½" x 42" strip, one cream 3½" x 42" strip, and one brown 3½" x 42" strip together as shown to make strip set F. Repeat with one brown 1½" x 20" strip, one cream 3½" x 20" strip, and one brown 3½" x 20" strip to make a half-strip set. Press the seam allowances toward the brown strips. Crosscut the strip sets into 36 segments, 1½" wide.

Strip set F.
Make 1½. Cut 36 segments.

11. Sew an F segment to opposite sides of a cream 1½" square. Press the seam allowances toward the F segments. Repeat to make a total of 18 units.

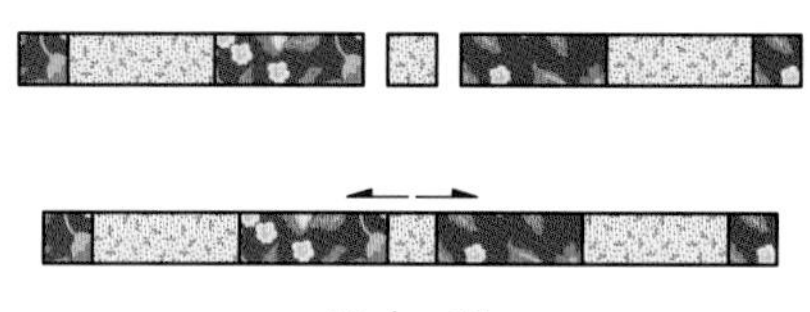
Make 18.

12. Sew an E unit to the sides of each unit from step 7. Press the seam allowances toward the E units. Add an F unit to the top and bottom of the step 7 units. Press the seam allowances toward the F units.

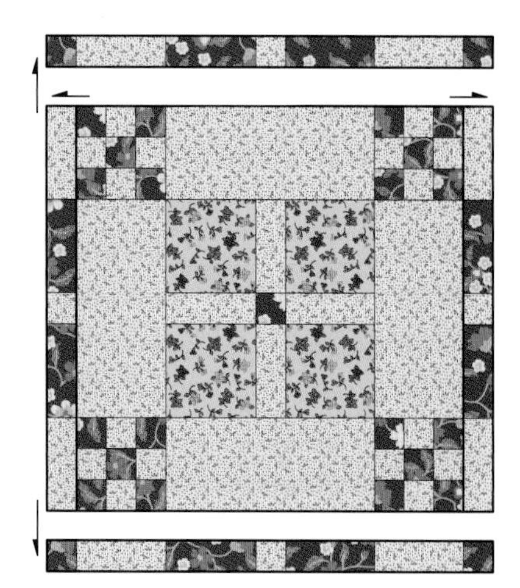
Make 9.

13. Join two cream 7½" x 42" strips and one brown 1½" x 42" strip together as shown to make strip set G. Press the seam allowances toward the brown strip. Crosscut the strip set into 18 segments, 1½" wide.

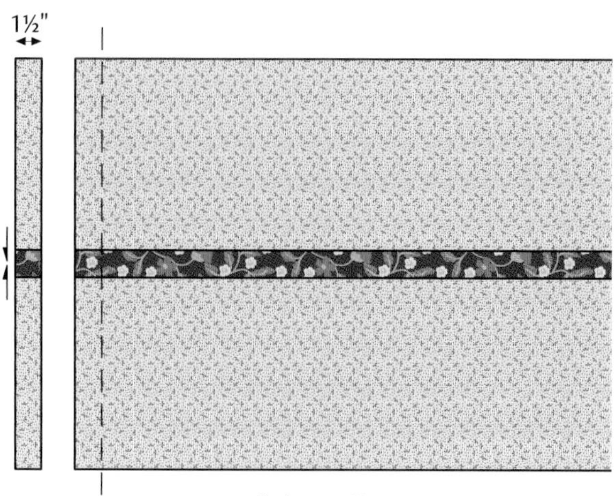

Strip set G.
Make 1. Cut 18 segments.

14. Join two brown 1½" x 42" strips and one cream 7½" x 42" strip together as shown to make strip set H. Press the seam allowances toward the brown strips. Crosscut the strip set into 18 segments, 1½" wide.

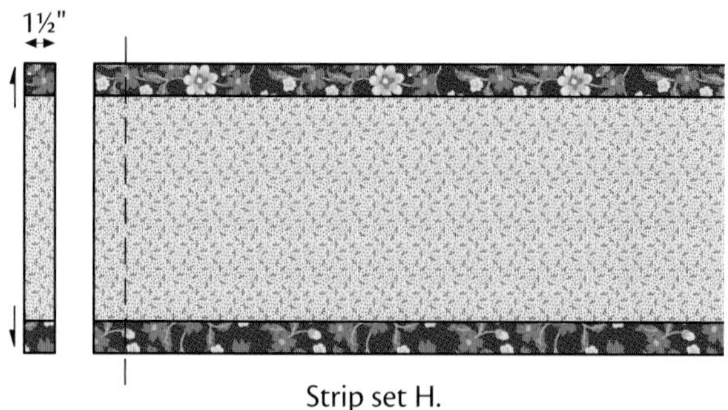

Strip set H.
Make 1. Cut 18 segments.

15. Join one brown 1½" x 42" strip and one cream 7½" x 42" strip as shown to make strip set I. Press the seam allowance toward the brown strip. Crosscut the strip set into 18 segments, 1½" wide.

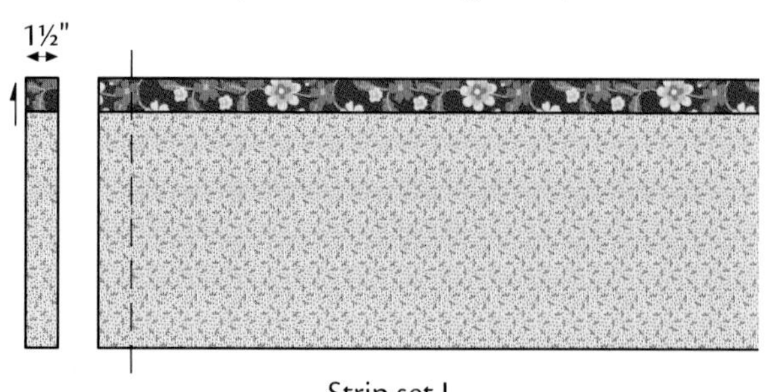

Strip set I.
Make 1. Cut 18 segments.

16. Sew each H segment to an I segment as shown. Press the seam allowances toward the H segments.

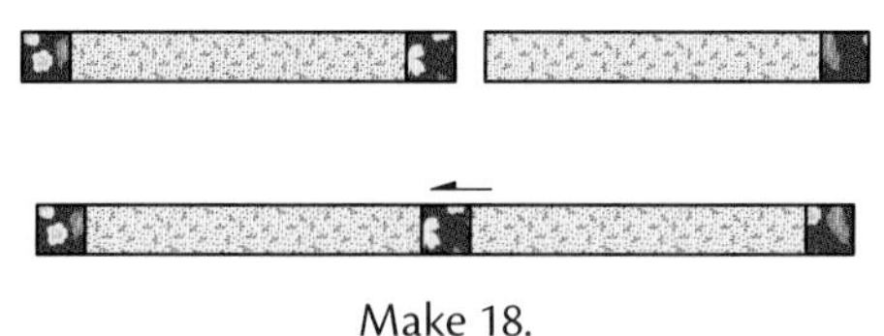

Make 18.

17. Sew a G segment to the sides of each unit from step 12. Press the seam allowances toward the G segments. Sew a unit from step 16 to the top and bottom of each unit from step 12 to complete the blocks. Press the seam allowances toward the unit from step 12.

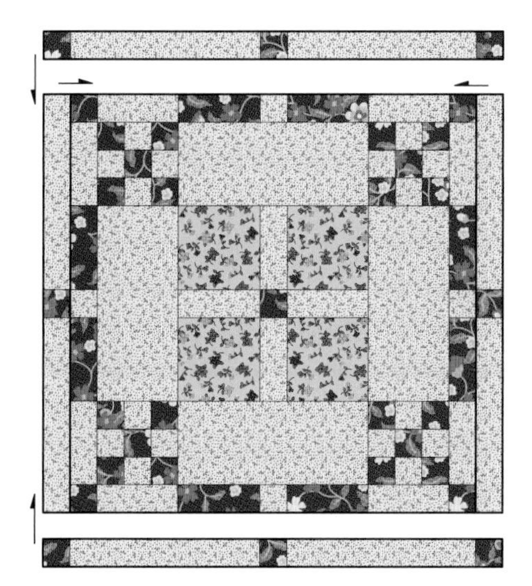

Make 9.

ASSEMBLING THE QUILT TOP

1. Sew four cream nine-patch units that you set aside earlier and three cream 3½" x 17½" pieces as shown to make a sashing row. Press the seam allowances toward the cream pieces. Repeat to make a total of four rows.

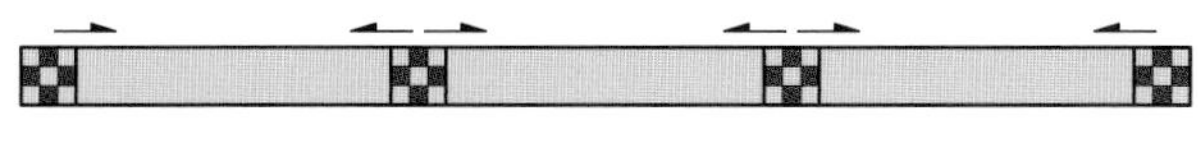

Make 4.

2. Sew three blocks and four cream 3½" x 17½" sashing strips together as shown to make a block row. Press the seam allowances toward the cream pieces. Repeat to make a total of three rows.

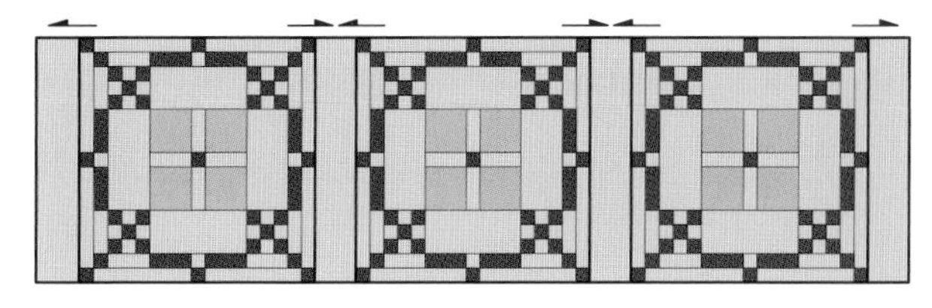

Make 3.

3. Refer to the quilt assembly diagram below to alternately lay out the block rows and sashing rows. Sew the rows together. Press the seam allowances in one direction.
4. Refer to "Adding Borders" on page 20 to add the cream 3½"-wide inner-border strips to the quilt top, piecing the strips as necessary. Repeat with the caramel print 3½"-wide middle-border strips, and then the aqua 6½"-wide outer-border strips.

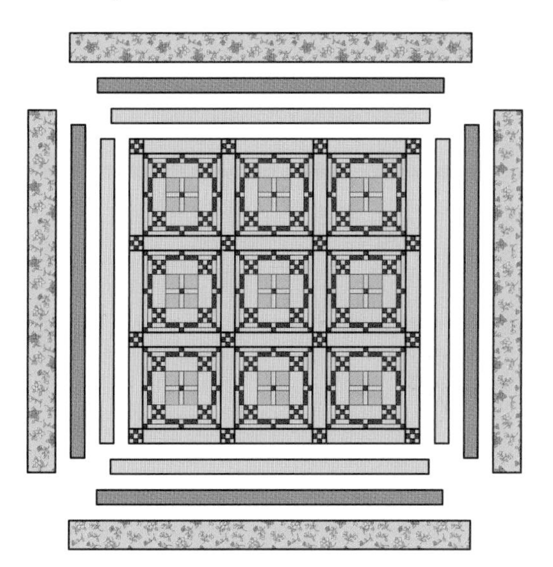

Quilt assembly

FINISHING THE QUILT

Refer to "Finishing Techniques" on page 21 for detailed instructions.

1. Layer the quilt top with batting and backing; baste.
2. Quilt as desired. Diana chose a wonderful allover feather design for this quilt. Because the main background fabric is printed with a small design, a lot of heirloom stitching would be lost on this quilt. A better choice to maintain the vintage look was to use an allover medium-sized feathery design.
3. Bind the quilt edges with the 2¼"-wide binding strips.

velvet romance pillow

Designed and sewn by Jackie Cate.

I love fabrics that are old fashioned and modern at the same time. The velvet I used as the center of this pillow is just that—a classic design in Fresh Vintage colors. I love the elegance of the velvet and crocheted lace combined with the simplicity and homespun feel of the wonderful gingham and tiny blue print. It gives a fresh, romantic taste to any bedroom.

—Jackie

Finished pillow size: 16" x 12"

MATERIALS

Yardages are based on 42"-wide fabrics.

1 fat quarter of aqua-and-green printed velvet for pillow center

1 fat quarter of aqua print for sides

1/8 yard of green gingham for flanges, piping, and backing

7/8 yard of 3"-wide flat crocheted lace

2 yards of 1/4" cotton cording for piping

16" x 12" pillow form

CUTTING

All measurements include 1/4"-wide seam allowances.

From the green gingham, cut:
1 piece, 12½" x 16½"

2 pieces, 2" x 12½"

From the aqua-and-green printed velvet, cut:
1 piece, 10½" x 12½"

From the lace, cut:
2 pieces, 12½" long

From the aqua print, cut:
2 pieces, 3½" x 12½"

MAKING THE PILLOW

1. Press the green gingham 2" x 12½" flange pieces in half lengthwise, wrong sides together.
2. Place the printed velvet piece on your work surface right side up with the 12½" edges along the sides. Layer the following pieces on each side, aligning the raw edges: lace, flange, and aqua print piece, wrong side up. Stitch the layers together along each side.

3. Press the seam allowances open. Press the flange toward the aqua piece and the lace toward the velvet piece on each side.
4. To make the piping, from the remainder of the green gingham, cut 2¼"-wide bias strips. You will need enough strips to make a strip approximately 65" long when pieced together. With the right side of the pieced bias strip out, fold the bias strip in half lengthwise over the cording. Line up the fabric raw edges so that the cord is in the center of the strip.
5. Using a zipper or cording foot, machine baste close to the cording, but not as close as you can, the entire length of the strip. You want to leave a little allowance so that when you sew the cording to the pillow cover, the basting stitches will not show. If you are using a zipper foot, move the needle so that it is to the left of the foot. For a piping foot, the piping will be under the groove of the foot and the raw edges of the fabric will be to the right.

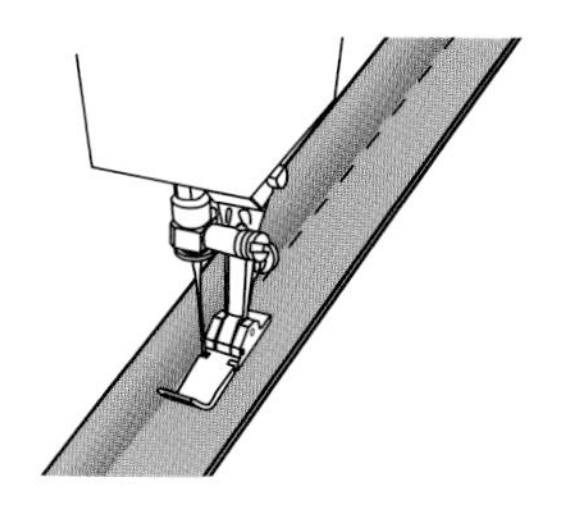

6. Trim the excess fabric ¼" from the basting stitches. The piping is now ready to be applied to the pillow cover edges.

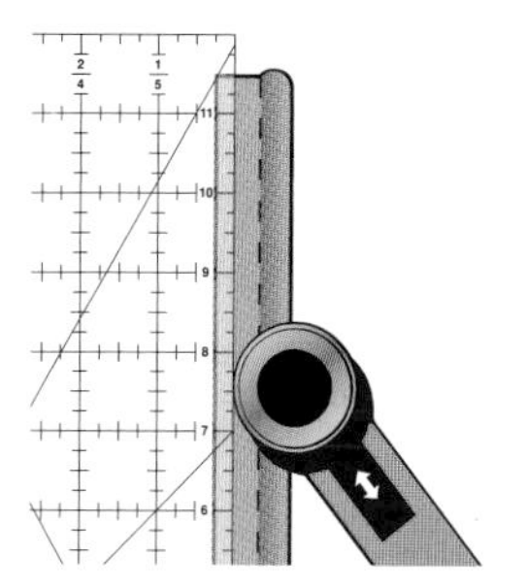

7. Pin the piping to the right side of the pillow cover, aligning the raw edges. If necessary, clip the piping seam allowance at the corners so that it lies flat.

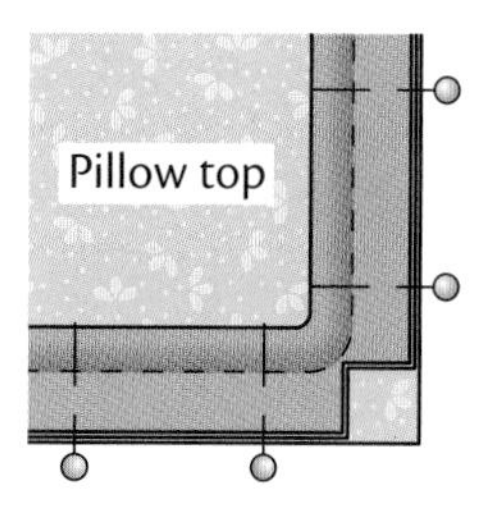

8. When you reach the starting point, trim the end of the piping so it overlaps the beginning about 1". Rip out about 1" of stitches on the end of the piping, exposing the cord inside. Trim the ends of the cording so they just touch and do not overlap. Press under the fabric on the end of the piping about ¼". Fold this edge over the ends of the cording so you have a finished edge. Baste the piping in place.

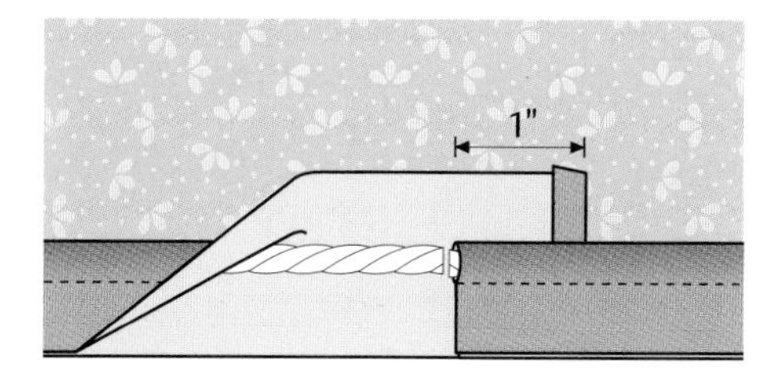

9. With right sides together, pin the gingham 12½" x 16½" piece to the pillow cover front, aligning raw edges. With your piping or zipper foot, stitch as close as you can to the piping all around the project, leaving a 6" to 8" opening on one side for turning.
10. Turn the pillow cover right side out. Press. Insert the pillow form through the opening. Whipstitch (see page 28) the opening closed.

lovely lavender sachets

Designed and sewn by Jackie Cate.

These lovelies are wonderful in a basket in your room or tucked away in a drawer to keep your clothes smelling sweet. Lavender is one of my favorite scents, and I love having these sweet sachets around my home giving off their gentle, relaxing fragrance. If you have a collection of those lovely charm squares, the small sachet is a great place to use them. Make a bunch and give them as gifts!

—Jackie

Finished large sachet size: 6" x 6"
Finished small sachet size: 4" x 4"

MATERIALS

These sachets are more interesting if you use a variety of different fabrics.

Large Sachet

2 squares, 6½" x 6½"

Two-hole flat buttons: ¾"-diameter and 1" diameter

22" of flat crocheted lace

2 tablespoons of dried lavender buds

Cotton stuffing

Small Sachet

4½" x 4½" square of fabric for bottom

4½" x 2½" piece of fabric for top

3½" x 2½" piece of fabric for top

1½" x 2½" piece of fabric for top

2½" x 2½" piece of fabric for covered button

Covered button kit for 1"-diameter button or any 1"-diameter button

1 tablespoon of dried lavender buds

Cotton stuffing

ASSEMBLING THE LARGE SACHET

1. Determine which fabric will be the top of the sachet. Position the lace on the right side of that square about 1" from the edge all around. At the corners, simply fold the lace back on itself to form a mitered look. Pin the lace in place and then machine or hand stitch through the center of the lace. If you are concerned about stability, you can stitch along the outer and inner edges.
2. Sew the two squares right sides together, leaving a 1½" opening on one side for turning and stuffing.
3. Turn the piece right side out. Stuff it with cotton batting and the lavender buds. Whipstitch the opening closed (see page 28).
4. Center the large button on the top of the sachet and the small button on the bottom. Stitch the buttons in place at the same time, pulling tightly to create a slight indentation at the center of the sachet. Once the buttons are secure, knot the ends of your thread and bury the knot inside the sachet.

ASSEMBLING THE SMALL SACHET

1. Sew the two smaller pieces of fabric together along the 2½" sides, right sides together; press the seam allowance in either direction. Sew the 4½" x 2½" piece of fabric to this unit along the 4½" side to create the top of the sachet. Press the seam allowance in either direction.
2. Sew the top and bottom pieces right sides together, leaving a 1" opening on one side for turning and stuffing. Turn the piece right side out.
3. If you are using a covered button, follow the instructions that came with the kit to cover the form with the 2½" square of fabric. Sew the covered button, or the regular button if you prefer, to the sachet front at the intersection where all the seams meet.
4. Stuff the piece with cotton batting and the lavender buds. Whipstitch the opening closed (see page 28).

a few of our favorite things

Designed and created by Janis Stob and Margaret Linderman.

On a recent impromptu road trip, we walked into a lovely antique treasure trove and found a soft roll of ticking tucked away in the corner of the store. Upon unrolling it, we discovered it had pockets—what could be better! We imagined so many different uses; perhaps a holder of all things magic for a busy laundry day, a place for all those bedroom tidbits, a spot for fabric inspirations. What could you organize with this little item?

—Janis and Margaret

Finished holder size: 21½" x 36"

MATERIALS

Yardages are based on 42"-wide fabrics, unless otherwise indicated.

1½ yards of striped fabric

1¼ yards of fabric for backing and binding

1 square, 10" x 10", *each* of 9 coordinating fabrics

⅜ yard of unbleached muslin for pocket lining

⅛ yard of contrasting fabric for pocket top flange

1½ yards of 34"-wide fusible batting

¾ yard of 22"-wide woven fusible interfacing (we used Form-Flex)

Wooden coat hanger

Chalk marker

CUTTING

All measurements include ¼"-wide seam allowances.

From the batting, cut:

1 piece, 9¼" x 21½"

1 piece, 21½" x 36¼"

From the striped fabric, cut*:

1 piece, 9¼" x 21½"

1 piece, 21½" x 36¼"

Cut pieces so the stripes run parallel to the 21½"-long edges.

From the fabric for backing and binding, cut:

3 strips, 2¼" x 42"

1 piece, 9¼" x 21½"

1 piece, 21½" x 36¼"

From the 9 coordinating fabric squares, cut:

6 squares, 8" x 8"

3 pieces, 9" x 8"

From the muslin, cut,

6 squares, 8" x 8"

3 pieces, 9" x 8"

From the interfacing, cut:

3 pieces, 8" x 24"

From the contrasting fabric for pocket flange, cut:

3 pieces, 1" x 24"

PREPARING THE FRONT AND BACK SECTIONS

1. Follow the manufacturer's instructions to fuse the batting pieces to the wrong side of the corresponding striped pieces.
2. Layer the backing and striped pieces as follows, aligning the 21½" edges along the top:
   backing 21½" x 36¼" piece, right side up;
   striped 21½" x 36¼" piece, wrong side up;
   striped 9¼" x 21½" piece, right side up;
   backing 9¼" x 21½" piece, wrong side up.
3. Find the center of the top edge. Make a mark 1" from both sides of the center. Place the hook of the wooden hanger between the two marks so that the highest point of the hanger shoulders is ¼" below the top edge of the fabric. Draw across the top of the hanger shoulders using a ruler to extend the angle all the way to the sides of the fabric. Remove the hanger and draw a line ¼" above that line. Cut on the marked line through all the layers.

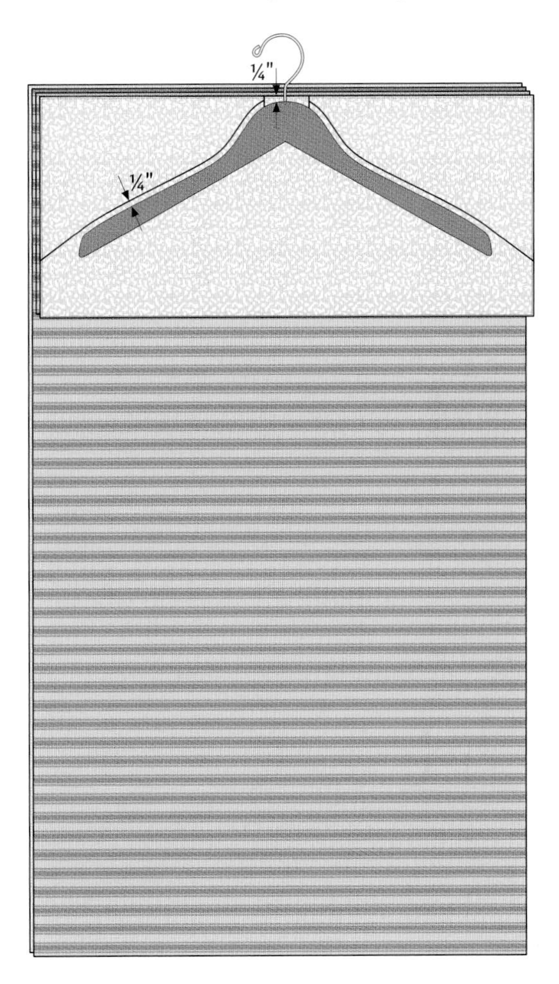

4. Carefully remove the top two pieces of the layered fabrics, keeping them together. These are for the back section. The longer pieces are for the front section.

ASSEMBLING THE ORGANIZER

1. With the right sides together as they were layered, stitch the front pieces together at the hanger opening as shown. Repeat with the back section. Press the seam allowances in opposite directions.

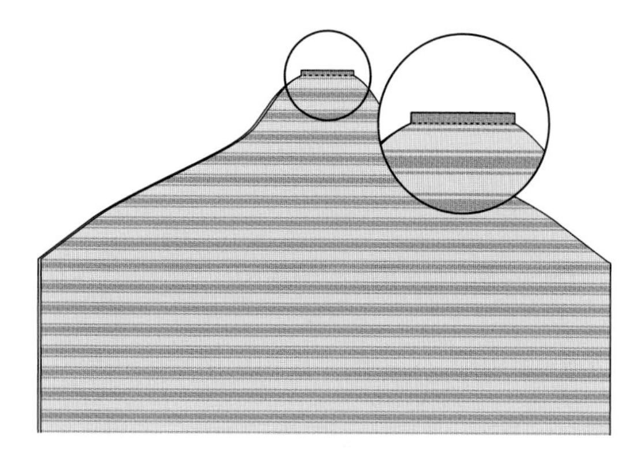

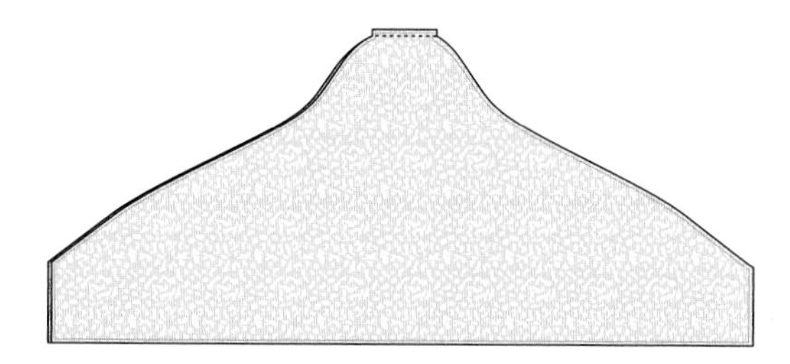

2. Open up the front and back sections and lay them flat, right sides together with the lining fabric sides facing and the striped fabric sides facing. Stitch along the shoulder areas as shown. Turn the pieces to the right side.

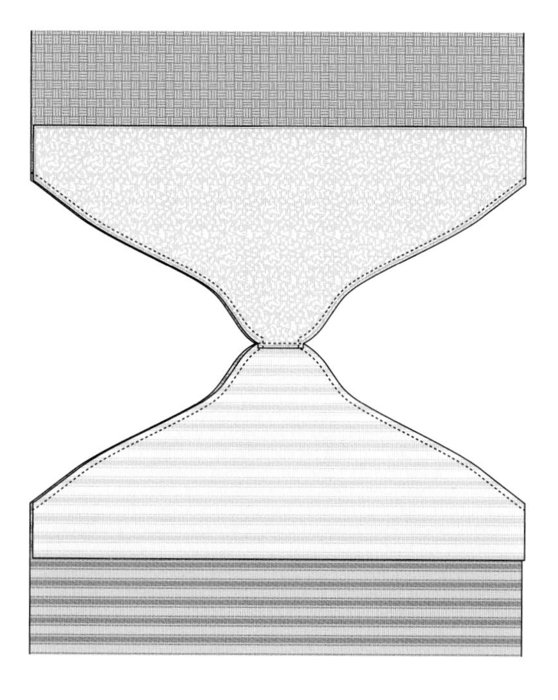

3. Fold each of the coordinating fabric 8" pocket squares in half right sides together. To make the bottom pleat, make a mark ½" from the fold and 1" long, measuring from the bottom edge. Stitch on the marked line, backstitching at the beginning and end. Fold each coordinating fabric 9" x 8" pocket piece in half right sides together to make a piece 8" x 4½". Mark and stitch each piece in the same manner as the squares. Repeat with the muslin 8" squares and 9" x 8" pieces.

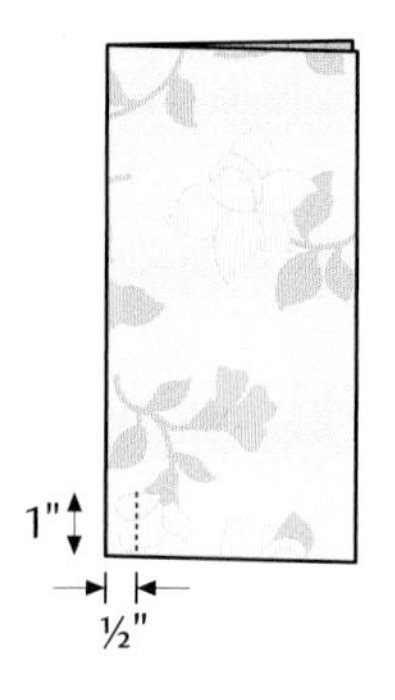

4. Stitch an 8" pocket square to the left and right edges of a 9" x 8" pocket piece, right sides together. Repeat to make a total of three rows. Press the seam allowances toward the outer pocket squares. Repeat with the muslin pieces to make a total of three lining rows. Press the seam allowances toward the middle pocket piece.

Make 3 rows from coordinating pieces and 3 rows from muslin pieces.

5. Follow the manufacturer's instructions to fuse the interfacing to the wrong side of each pocket row. Trim away any excess around the edges.

6. Fold each flange 1" x 24" piece in half, wrong sides together. Place a flange strip on the right side of a pocket row, aligning the raw edges. Place a lining row over the pocket row and flange, right sides together. Sew along the top edge only. Turn the pocket unit to the right side. Repeat to make a total of three lined pocket units.

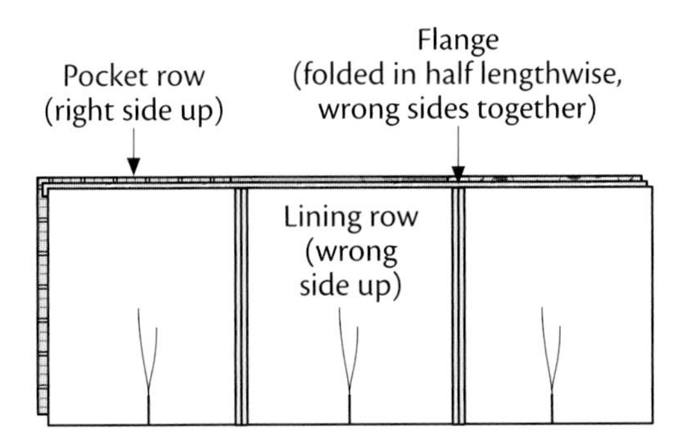

7. Position a pocket unit along the bottom edge of the front section, aligning the bottom and side edges; pin in place. Arrange and pin the center pocket so the seam lines are straight and parallel to the sides. There will be excess fabric along the top edge of the pockets because of the pleat. Stitch in the ditch of the center pocket seam lines, and then stitch across the bottom and side edges.

8. Measure and chalk-mark 2" up from the top of the bottom pocket unit flange. Lay the bottom edge of a pocket unit face down on this line and stitch through all layers along the bottom edge. Go over the stitching line to reinforce it. Flip up the pocket unit and stitch it in place as you did for the bottom pocket unit.

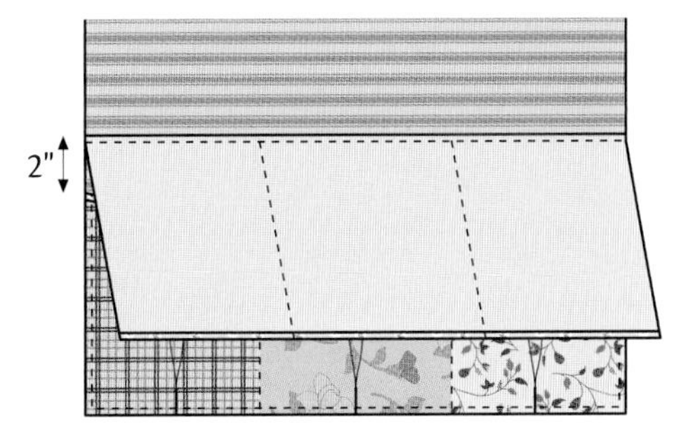

9. Measure and chalk-mark 1¾" up from the top of the center pocket unit flange. Repeat step 8 to sew the unit in place, being careful not to catch the back section in the stitching.

FINISHING THE ORGANIZER

1. Refer to "Binding" on page 22 to bind the bottom edge of the back section using one of the 2¼" x 42" binding strips.
2. Insert the hanger between the front and back sections, and then pin the front and back sections together along the sides. Piece the remaining binding strips together to make one long strip. Refer to the photo on page 104 to bind the front section straight side edges and bottom edge, catching the back section in the side binding.

dreaming journal

Designed and created by Janis Stob and Margaret Linderman.

Because dreams inspire us, we always have a book handy to jot down thoughts, colors, and feelings from those dreams. This journal is great because you can replace the book inside when it is filled up. A gift of a journal like this will encourage another to capture those moments, sketches, and dreams.

—Janis and Margaret

Finished size: To fit a 7½" x 9¾" composition book

MATERIALS

Yardages are based on 42"-wide fabrics.

⅜ yard of fabric for outer cover

⅜ yard of coordinating fabric for inner cover and appliqué flanges

⅜ yard of neutral-colored flannel (this will be used in place of batting)

⅛ yard of contrasting fabric for cover flanges and facing

1 fat quarter of print for appliqué background and frame backing

3" x 10" piece of felted wool to match outer cover fabric for "dream" appliqué

Cream silk thread

CUTTING

All measurements include ¼"-wide seam allowances.

From the fat quarter of print, cut:

1 piece, 4" x 6½"

1 piece, 5" x 7½"

From the neutral-colored flannel, cut:

1 piece, 4" x 6½"

1 piece 10½" x 24"

From the coordinating fabric, cut:

2 pieces, 1" x 4"

2 pieces, 1" x 7½"

1 piece 10½" x 24"

From the fabric for outer cover, cut:

1 piece, 10½" x 24"

From the contrasting fabric, cut:

2 strips, 1" x 15½"

2 strips, 1¼" x 9½"

MAKING THE APPLIQUÉD PIECE

1. Refer to "Appliqué" on page 17 and use the patterns below to cut out the appliqués from the wool fabric.
2. Lay a print 4" x 6½" piece over the flannel 4" x 6½" piece, right side up. This is to add some depth to the piece. Position the appliqué letters on the layered pieces to spell "dream" and appliqué them in place with the silk thread, stitching through both layers.
3. Stitch the 1" x 4" pieces to the sides of the appliquéd piece. Sew the 1" x 7½" pieces to the top and bottom of the appliquéd piece.

4. Lay the solid 5" x 7½" backing piece over the appliquéd piece, right sides together. Stitch completely around the piece. Trim the corners. Cut a slit about 3" long in the backing piece only and turn the piece right side out through the slit. Push out the corners and press.

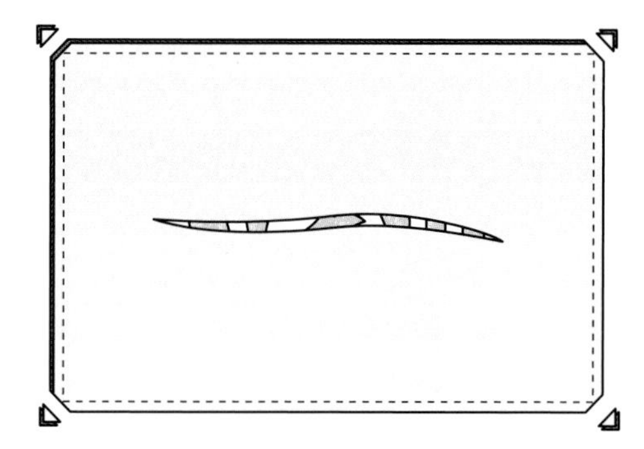

ASSEMBLING THE COVER

1. Place the flannel piece on your work surface. Layer the outer cover piece over it right side up. Place the coordinating fabric 10½" x 24" piece over the outer cover piece wrong side up. Make sure all the edges are aligned. Stitch the short edges together. Turn the piece right side out. Fold the piece in half crosswise so the finished ends meet; pin mark the top and bottom edges at the fold to mark the center.
2. Referring to "Le Journal de Paris" on page 90, repeat steps 2 and 3 to create the flanges from the contrasting fabric 1" x 15½" pieces and apply them to the cover pieces. Repeat step 4, measuring in 8" to create the flaps. Repeat steps 5 and 6 with the contrasting fabric 1¼" x 9½" pieces to make and apply the facing pieces. Repeat step 7 to stitch the appliquéd piece to the cover front, being careful not to stitch through the flap.

Cut 1 of each piece.

HÔTEL CARPEAUX
love
mistletoe
A Story Book
ORCHARD
PURE
MILK
PARIS